Pull Back

YOUR

Power

The ground-breaking
code to unlocking
profound confidence
and soaring success for
aspirational women

Anne Whitehouse PhD

RETHINK PRESS

First published in Great Britain in 2019
by Rethink Press (www.rethinkpress.com)

© Copyright Anne Whitehouse

Cover image and illustrations © Anne Whitehouse

Praise

'I cannot believe I had to wait until the age of
seventy before I could read this incredible book!
I hope it becomes compulsory reading for every
girl on the planet by the age of twelve, so they can
have this knowledge and wisdom right from the
beginning. This book creates the most perfect stone
bridge for all women. Anne's brilliance, wisdom and
understanding shimmers through each sentence. I
wish my mother could have read this and I hope all
our daughters will read it.'
— **Melissie Jolly**, Founder of Colour Mirrors

'This book will resonate with professional women
and is a must read for those who want to regain
their female power. I am astonished at how this book
resonated with me and my experiences. This book
enabled me to understand why I have been held
back and what was the root cause. Anne, through
her engaging writing style, has made me think that
at times she is speaking to me directly, so much so
that I thought I was having a one-to-one consultation
with her! This book is rich in experiences. There are
plenty of exercises and advice which will help you to
reactivate your female power. This is a fabulous book
if you truly want to find your real self, and regain
confidence and self-esteem.'
— **Barbara Bogusz**, University Lecturer in Law

'The reality is that both women and men are seeking a softer feminine power to lead their communities, corporations and countries. This book is arriving at a crucial time when we desperately need to find out how to let go of the old ways, where all we knew was based on patriarchal systems encoded into our psyche. This book suggests gentle, graceful ways to free ourselves from the past and, instead of being angry, move forward knowing how to be authentically and genuinely empowered for success.'
   — **Moira Bush**, host of *The Magenta Show*

'This is the book of all books for professional women who have been impacted by multiple generations of patriarchy. Anne valiantly dismantles our patriarchal systems, ideologies and beliefs, to expose women to the truth of their innate power and potential, without defaulting to masculinised skills in order to be considered equal. Her revolutionary findings, and personal experiences, reveal the underlying male dominance and excessive female subordination in the workforce, particularly among those women seeking to ascend the ladder while maintaining work–life balance. Women who read this book have the inside track to effecting transformation and breaking the dysfunctional power cycle between the sexes.'
   — **Sophia Marsh-Ochsner**, marketing agency
   owner and success coach

'It is a rare gift to write well about our innermost feelings and what holds us back. Through reading this book I have been captivated and encouraged to start my own journey to empowerment. Thank you, Anne, for sharing your wisdom and guidance. I urge anyone to forget anything else on the subject and grab a copy of this book. I absolutely love it!'
— **Sally Barnett**, Barrister and
Head of Chambers

'*Pull Back Your Power* is exciting, riveting reading. With brilliantly clear guidance and an engaging style that will have you hooked from the first page, this book sets out exactly what has been stopping you living your best, most authentic life and shows you how to go about changing that. It sets out precise and empowering steps for any woman who has been through the bewildering experience of being held back, blocked or thwarted in any aspect of her life or career. Anne's passion for her topic is inspirational and shines through every page. Her wisdom and guidance are superb, and the combination of the logical and the scientific with subtle yet extraordinary energy tools makes empowering yourself not only possible but inevitable.'
— **Korani Connolly**, author and owner of
Korani Light Centre

'When I read *Pull Back Your Power*, my depression had got me into a state where I could not do anything anymore and was terrified to go to work. Anne's book gave me a glimmer of hope that perhaps she could help me, when nothing else I'd tried had really helped. It turned out that I did have many of the blocks she describes in the book, and after working through this, I was able to go to work again. I learned how to pull back my power. While not everything can be solved at once, I feel as if I've finally found a way of recovering.

    — **Dr Julia Goedecke**, University Teaching Fellow in Mathematics

'In my work empowering entrepreneurs to stand out and bring their visions to the world, I've seen brilliant women struggle with lack of confidence, and this limits their success. Anne's book *Pull Back Your Power* provides a revolutionary solution. She not only explains precisely how the legacy of the past still sabotages women, but provides the tools needed to enable them to step into the limelight and achieve the success they deserve.'

    — **Marisa Murgatroyd**, founder of Live Your Message

For my mother, Ruth,
my grandmothers, Lily and Alice,
and for my beloved daughter, Rebecca.
Although she only lived seven short years,
she was the epitome of feminine confidence,
magic and power – a true fairy princess.

To Dron
with love and
best wishes

[signature]

5th August 2020

Contents

Foreword

'**M**agical and utterly compelling.'

If you are a woman who has ever felt exhausted or thwarted, despite your best efforts to succeed, finally, you have the stunning explanation why. I recognised myself (as well as many of my professional sisters) amongst the five typical female archetypes us 'power women' are subconsciously drawn into – none of which are truly empowering – and finally understood how and why my life had always felt like such a battle. In this wonderfully liberating book, Anne also offers a series of beautiful and powerfully transformative practical tools to assist us in our collective journey toward the 'Evolved Feminine'.

I'd like to explain why I have described this book as 'magical and utterly compelling'. But first, some context.

I'd agreed to review the draft and write a testimonial, provided a hard copy was sent to me. I then forgot all about it until I returned from holiday to a card asking me to collect a 'to be signed for' delivery at the sorting office, which I did later that day.

I then headed up to the local church and sat in stillness for a while, offering up a few silent prayers. Why did it feel as if my life was in the doldrums? Where along the way had I so spectacularly lost my mojo? How come the only tasks I felt able to complete competently and without anxiety these days were housework and cooking?

'Please, send me some help and guidance.'

The answer was sitting right there, in the unopened envelope on the pew next to me. Once I started reading the manuscript later that day I could not stop until I reached the end. This book perfectly explained 'The Beast' I had been up against my entire life without ever being consciously aware of it – and I am someone who has truly gone deep with all sorts of transformational processes, exploring every aspect of childhood trauma, delving into the various Shadow aspects of myself, even going on spiritual pilgrimages to Peru to experience plant medicine with the shamans. I knew I had to be missing something, but I didn't know what.

My life as a professional woman has always been in the world of money and business. I worked my way up in accountancy and then created my own company, Red Letter Days, at the age of twenty-four, building it up into an award-winning multimillion-pound turn-over market-leading brand, only to lose it fourteen years later to a series of calamities. Thanks to my TV fame as one of the 'Dragons' on the first two series of the BBC's acclaimed business show Dragons' Den, I was pretty much annihilated by the media.

Despite many and varied attempts to get my life back on track, everything seemed to turn to dust – especially as I started to unplug from the masculine warrior energy that had been driving me for so many years (I grew up with four brothers, so had battle training). I also trained in trauma healing skills and it dawned on me just how many years I had been living in full 'predator alert', in a soup of adrenaline.

It seems to me that we are currently at a crucial turning point, where it is vital that women root out every last piece of patriarchal programming, the deeply ingrained legacy of so many years of male dominance. Yet we will not achieve this unless we realise just how radically our power has been undermined.

This book explains 'The Beast' we are up against, and how we can transmute and transcend it. This is precious, essential reading for every woman striving to be successful in a man's world and I am so grateful for the many hours of meticulous, logical research Anne has put in to create it. I know that it will inspire you as much as it did me.

Rachel Elnaugh
Entrepreneur

Introduction

Once upon a time, a young girl called Grace went out into the world. She had been promised a fairy tale, a bright future in the Palace of Success. A future of equality and opportunity. A future where she was respected and her gifts were valued, where she could make her dreams come true if she worked hard. Skipping along the path, she felt excited, curious and eager to prove her worth. After a few miles, she met a young man; we'll call him George. They got chatting, and they soon realised they had much in common – shared goals, qualifications, interests and gifts – and since they were both destined for the palace, they decided to travel together.

Just as things were looking rosy, they came to a fork in the road, guarded by Old Man Status Quo. He ushered George down the right-hand path, which was brightly lit and covered with flowers. 'Can't I take that path, too?' asked Grace. 'The other path goes through the forest.' 'No!' said Status Quo. 'You must take the left-hand path.'

So Grace and George bade each other farewell and agreed to rendezvous at the palace.

Now, Grace was a twenty-first-century girl, who believed in equality, her rights and her independence, and she didn't believe in monsters, so she took a deep breath and set off into the forest. But little did she know that along her path, beasts really were lurking in the shadows, and huge obstacles really would block her way – obstacles and beasts that George would never have to deal with.

And so our story begins…

Have you ever been in a situation where you have felt invisible, or worse, relegated to nothing more than someone to serve tea in a room where you are in fact 'the expert'?

Did you believe that if you got an education, qualified and became an authority in your field, you would be realising your potential? But then, once you got there, you didn't feel good enough, couldn't put yourself and your ideas forward, and didn't shine when you wanted to?

Or worse, does life feel like an exam where perfection is the standard? Do you feel judged, and dread criticism? Do your stress and anxiety seem way out of proportion and everyday events feel like ordeals? Are you driven to push yourself harder and harder, the ease and confidence your abilities should give you remaining elusive?

Or maybe you've achieved great things, built a business or launched your mission, but then, out of the blue, money issues, anxiety and glass ceilings have brought everything crashing down. Did you think that in this modern society you would be free to express your gifts and achieve everything you are capable of?

Something is going on under the surface; something that sabotages women specifically. Something that isn't fully acknowledged or understood. Something the conventional world doesn't understand.

In recent years there have been some brilliant books spotlighting the confidence gap between women and men (Kay and Shipman, 2014), the way in which women don't ask for what they want and deserve (Babcock and Laschever, 2008), and the way data collection is biased against women (Criado Perez, 2019). We can all see that the unconscious bias persists. However, in this book I'm going beyond these things. I'm going to show you precisely what is happening under the surface, in our minds and in our society, to create these effects. I'm going to explain the very real damage, way beyond promotions and salaries, that this phenomenon does to your life and your well-being. But most importantly, this book will show you how to free yourself to shine, succeed and embody your true power in the world.

Did you start out in life with excitement and optimism? I certainly did. The trouble was that, as a woman, my journey to the Palace of Success was fraught with obstacles, hidden dangers and challenges that my male counterparts never had to overcome; obstacles they didn't even realise existed, and some perils that they actively created. Those challenges were enormous and changed everything for me, and many women like me.

After a glowing eight years at Cambridge, at the age of twenty-six, I found myself as the youngest university lecturer in the UK that year, in a male-dominated engineering department. I was idealistic and determined. I was on a mission to show the world that, as a woman, and in my case a very feminine woman, I could succeed in this masculine environment. I was no warrior. I was sensitive and quiet, passionate and motivated, a deep thinker. With long hair down to my waist, dangly earrings and long silk skirts, I entered the world of mechanical engineering labs, locker-room innuendo, beer and cricket matches. I had gained entry to the infamous 'Boys' Club'.

What happened next could fill a few volumes at least. Suffice it to say, it all began to go wrong practically from day one. I never felt good enough, despite my credentials being equal to those of every man there. I never felt confident. I always felt under attack. I always felt vulnerable. I struggled to speak up with my colleagues. I began to push myself harder and harder. Research grants came in, papers were published, I received excellent feedback from my students, yet still I didn't feel I belonged. Stress and anxiety took hold. Distasteful experiences with various men I encountered (I am sure, in this #metoo era, you can imagine the type of thing I'm referring to) undermined me further. Then came chronic insomnia and endless infections, which eventually spiralled into chronic fatigue syndrome.

At the age of thirty-two, my scientific career was over.

What had happened? Why had I been unable to thrive in a career for which I was eminently qualified? Why had everything collapsed?

One thing is certain, when I left my lectureship in 2001, I believed that there was something fundamentally wrong with me. Something that made me intrinsically weak, not capable of cutting it out in the world. All my dreams had been shattered because something inside me had imploded and caused everything to self-destruct.

If you are a motivated, intelligent woman who wants to succeed and prove herself – maybe in a conventional career like me; maybe as an entrepreneur or woman who wants to see her vision manifested in the world; maybe as an actress, artist or another career in the public eye – you will come across the same undermining obstacles as I did, in one guise or another. Very likely, you already have.

As we aspirational women push forward, we find ourselves being undermined – subtly, at first, but over time the problem grows. This leads to burnout, anxiety and stress, though on the surface the external landscape continues to improve for women. Even those women who are warrior types often find their success only lasts a certain amount of time before things come crashing down.

I've lost count of the amazing, gifted women I've worked with who are held back by not feeling good enough and by a reluctance to put themselves into the limelight. Women who, despite their passion and abilities, still hold back. I've also seen many women achieve in spite of huge obstacles only to then find things begin to crumble once they reach a certain level of success.

Something is holding us back, something huge. Something the world doesn't acknowledge, yet we feel it eating away at us from the inside. I vowed to work out what it was, and how to change it. This became my life's mission. So started my second career as a Life Alchemist. From metallurgist to alchemist – quite a transition!

I'm no tree-hugging hippy. I started off firmly rooted in the tangible world, with my PhD in metal matrix composites. However, when this mindset failed me, I was forced to expand my horizons into what I had previously believed impossible. I trained with the best and became an expert in subconscious mind reprogramming. When the existing healing modalities also failed to give me what I needed, I started from scratch. I pushed barriers and, with my scientific approach, I tested, experimented, refused to take 'impossible' for an answer, and gradually developed a completely new way of looking at things, and a revolutionary new set of tools. I became my guinea pig. My techniques worked, not only on myself but on my clients and students too. Here we are, eighteen years after I left that lectureship, and I've worked it out. I now know why I reacted that way, and I know how to change things and prevent other women from going through what I did.

What you'll find in this book is new; I've not only identified the true roots of our problem, I've worked out how to change them. If you follow this book through, take on board the big picture understanding, and do the exercises I give you, you will begin to level the energetic playing field and feel differently about your life.

The first section will take you on a journey deep into the real reasons why women continue to be held back. The second section is your definitive guide to counteracting these effects and will put you firmly on the path back to reactivating your female powers, where your natural self-esteem and confidence can safely shine.

It's about time all women were truly free to express who we are, our gifts, talents, mission and leadership in the world, so let's make it happen. All you need is an open mind, motivation and the belief that you deserve to fulfil your true potential.

There is a beast lurking in the shadows, sabotaging your wellbeing and success.

This is a book for pioneering women. If you're a woman who's tried to succeed the conventional way, but has still ended up struggling, blocked and undermined, then it's time for you to do what I did: start thinking outside the box.

By playing life according to the old rules, women can't truly win the game. We can only react, compensate and survive. We won't be genuinely free to shine until the old paradigm is fully unmasked and deactivated.

This takes courage, a willingness to break the rules and the resilience to keep going against the status quo.

It's time for a new way of being that creates a truly level playing field for women. It's time for aspirational women like us to build the power foundation we need for success, happiness and wellbeing.

If you're ready to be part of this, join me on the journey into a new world.

- Power foundation
- Zero energetic entitlement
- forbidden - Submission
-

PART ONE
THE REAL PROBLEM

This is a tale of two worlds: our familiar, 3D world and the hidden energetic world beneath. To master the first, you must confront and unravel the second.

You have within you the potential to be truly amazing, as yourself, and you have an absolute right to create the life you want, for yourself. All of your powers (and I use the plural intentionally here) have value and contribute to the whole you. At the moment, your true power has been blocked and sabotaged in ways you are unaware of, just because you are female. My purpose here is to enable you to unlock that power, so you can embody your unique magnificence. To achieve this, we now embark on a journey deep into the shadow of our society, to unmask that hidden sabotage and get you back on the path to becoming all that you can be.

1

The Downward Spiral

Grace had been brought up in an equal-opportunities household and had naturally assumed that the world would be the same. It had simply never occurred to her before that she would be treated differently. Now, though, as she ripped her sleeves on brambles and stumbled over tree roots, new thoughts began to form. What made George more special than her? What made her less deserving of the flowery path? One thing was certain, she was going to prove that she was just as good, no matter what it took.

It is 1998 and I am sitting in my doctor's office feeling dreadful. Low-grade fever and a sore throat have persisted for about six months now. I can hardly find the energy to walk. My body feels poisoned. Despair, panic, fear and anxiety fill my mind and body. I am falling apart. Dr Davis looks me straight in the eyes wearing an expression that says all too clearly that he's seen this all before. 'Listen to me, Anne,' he says.

'You are never going to be able to do this job without it making you ill. It's not a question of whether you can do the job itself, the environment in that engineering department is destroying you.'

Unfortunately, I didn't listen to him and soldiered on for another three years before I was forced to resign. By that time, I'd not only lost the career I'd worked so hard for, I'd also ruined my health.

Not my best decision, if I'm honest.

The false promise

As young women, we are promised a brave new world – a world in which we have equal rights with men, rights to education and opportunity. We look forward to a future where we can have any career we choose, where we can enjoy equality with our husbands and partners, share the household duties, delay our families until we've established ourselves, and take our rightful place in the world. A place we know we are entitled to because of our natural intelligence, motivation and hard work. Under the surface we have a burning desire to right the injustices of the past that deprived our mothers, grandmothers and great-grandmothers of these freedoms.

Isn't this what you hoped for? Didn't you think that with equal opportunity rights being enshrined in law across the western world, this would be possible?

We start out in our careers with the belief that we can do it, that we are good enough, that we are entitled to be there, that we will be able to perform to our true potential.

How do we react out in the world?

Innocently believing this, out we go into the world, ready and eager to achieve the success we rightly deserve. Maybe you choose a conventional career, like me: academic, accountant, doctor, actuary. Maybe you decide to launch your own business and become a wildly successful female entrepreneur. Or maybe your dream is to act on the stage with the Royal Shakespeare Company, or walk down the red carpet to great acclaim.

Whichever path you choose, the reality turns out to be completely different.

When you get into that environment, the one you are supposedly qualified to be in, it all falls apart. Maybe on the surface, everything looks completely fine, and the world sees your competence and achievements, but inside you simply don't feel it.[1] You don't feel good enough, even though you are. Maybe you can't speak up. You don't promote yourself. You let others speak over you in meetings. If you do push yourself

---

1   Katty Kay and Claire Shipman present many studies that confirm these trends in their book *The Confidence Code* (2014).

forward, it comes with hideous pangs of anxiety in your stomach, sleepless nights, a need to screw up your courage. Everything that should be normal, and easily within your scope, instead feels like a terrible trial. Life becomes about surviving the next ordeal. Stress ramps up. Anxiety ramps up. Wellbeing and happiness go downhill. Frustration emerges. Illness becomes chronic. Depression sets in. It's a complete nightmare.

The problem doesn't always show itself in this way. Perhaps you feel confident enough but, every way you turn, resistance and glass ceilings block your progress. You feel as if every step forward has you pushing against a concrete wall.

Do you feel the inner conflict, that endless push–pull? You desperately want to shine and fulfil your purpose or mission, but at the same time, you feel strapped into an invisible straitjacket that is consistently holding you back. You want to move but you can't. There just seems no way to break through these barriers.

The way it ends up will, of course, depend upon your character, constitution and circumstances. Suffice it to say that mental health issues, chronic fatigue, fibromyalgia, migraines, weight gain, digestive issues, eating disorders and body image problems, and other debilitating conditions feature frequently.[2] Even if

---

2   Many factors can contribute to whether someone develops these health conditions; however, I have found that they are frequently part of the female stress picture.

your physical health is not affected, the pain of not performing to your highest capability, of seeing less talented people surpass you, and of not achieving everything you know you're capable of, is just awful.

The result: frustration and suffering for you, while the world misses out on everything you have to offer. Everything you could be and could create is blocked, never to be realised. Meanwhile, you destroy yourself from within.

'Get some vitamin C and go for a run!' I was told. Unbelievably dismissive, when my entire life was falling apart. To me, it felt as if I had fallen into a bottomless pit and, to make matters worse, most of the people around me seemed oblivious to its existence. It's as if they were all standing on solid ground while I was falling into a black hole, and nobody could see there was nothing holding me up.

The inevitable conclusion

If these are the only facts at your disposal, there is only one logical conclusion you can make. You aren't good enough. You can't hack it. While your male counterparts, and indeed the female warrior types, seemingly sail along, effortlessly promoting themselves, often far beyond their true capabilities, you hold back, agonising over the smallest thing. In this world where so many seem to thrive and fulfil their potential, you struggle. You feel anxious in situations that don't warrant it. You hold back where you should shine. You sabotage yourself left, right and centre, and the more you try, the more you push yourself, the worse it seems to get.

The conclusion? You must be intrinsically and fundamentally flawed. You must be weak and pathetic. Worse, you have somehow let down the 'sisterhood' by not being the warrior woman you are 'meant to be' in this world.

Here is where the downward spiral of doom begins to escalate. The more you feel you aren't good enough, the more you push yourself to try harder. The more you push yourself, the more your destructive perfectionism tells you that nothing you do is good enough. Instead, self-criticism, endless regurgitating of past events and agonising over possible futures take all the joy out of life. And so the cycle continues, until something breaks. And indeed something will break. Your health, your relationships, your world. Take your pick.

There's nothing wrong with you

What if I told you there's nothing wrong with you? Let's say that again. There is nothing wrong with you. What if I told you that there's a good reason why you feel and react the way you do? Not only that, when you fully understand the extent of the issue, you'll realise how utterly amazing and courageous you are for having got this far.

Trust me. You'll realise once and for all that you, and I, and all women on this path, are quite phenomenal.

A fresh start

I've designed this book to take you on a journey through time and space, and it will give you a short-cut to what took me over twenty years to understand. It's a journey that will give you both the information and the tools you need to create real changes in the way you feel and react to life.

From this point on, we are starting again with a new premise. I am a scientist, and I don't think in a fluffy way. The only approach is to analyse the situation properly, so let's do exactly that.

It's a fact that many women suffer the same sort of stress reaction to life as I did. It occurs far too frequently for it to be simply a figment of our imagination. It cannot be us over-reacting, being over-sensitive or attention-seeking. This would defy logic. Yet, on the surface, our reaction does appear to be out of proportion.

The inevitable scientific conclusion is that there must be a factor which hasn't been taken into account; a factor which has a fundamental effect on the way we react mentally, emotionally and physically. From now on, we will assume the existence of that unknown 'Factor X'. We will identify its roots. We will then find a way to negate its effects upon us and a way to free ourselves so that the problem goes away. Here is our equation:

$$\text{Normal life} + \text{Factor } X = \frac{\text{High}}{\text{stress}} + \frac{\text{Feeling not}}{\text{good enough}}$$

Now, let's solve it. Sound good? Great. Let's get started.

From this point onwards, I want you to get a big metaphorical red pen and cross out all those self-destroying assumptions and conclusions you have made about yourself. The ones that are currently sitting like poison in your mind.

The fact is, you haven't had all the information. Without all the information your conclusions have been flawed. You have falsely accused yourself of being useless, not good enough; a fake and a fraud; a weak, pathetic woman. This is all rubbish, so cross those conclusions out. Go on, now. Cross them out. Good.

Now, step two, do the same thing with all the conclusions you made about what you were dealing with. Trust me when I tell you that you have only been aware of a fraction of the real challenges you've been fighting. Scrub all that out, too.

Let's start afresh with a lovely blank canvas. There are some facts about you that you can acknowledge: your natural abilities, your dedication, your qualifications, your creativity, your imagination, your compassion and kindness, your intelligence, your sense of humour, your perseverance, your resilience. The list could go on and on. For now, I want you to take a fresh look at who you are and what you have achieved. If you have difficulties seeing these qualities in yourself, imagine you're a stranger reading a CV of your life so far. You'll be amazed at just how impressive you are.

Our task is to enable you not only to know and feel that worth, in every cell of your body, but to live it out in the world – in your career, your intimate relationships, with your family – so that you no longer hold back, but allow all those gifts to shine and be fully expressed in all their glory. It's not an impossible dream; it's achievable with the right tools.

I'm eager to get on to more exciting discoveries, but we need to do this properly, so bear with me for a moment. Before we go any further down the rabbit hole, we need to set the stage and create the mindset you'll need to get the most out of this journey.

The Beast

There's a beast lurking under the surface of your life that's been sabotaging you without you knowing it.

Ignorance is not bliss. Before you can free yourself, you first need to understand this Beast: what it is, why it is there, how it has been impacting you. Only then can you transform your life.

The starting point of your journey is your subconscious mind. You may be familiar with subconscious limiting beliefs, but let me assure you, on this journey we are going much, much deeper. Changing those limiting beliefs does not solve our problems, but they are the reason we get locked in the downward spiral.

There's one thing I want you to take on board right now, because it's essential if you want to free yourself from this trap and open up your life to wellbeing and success. The beliefs and motivations you are aware of in your conscious mind are completely different from those in your subconscious.

Let me emphasise one thing: you are not aware of what your subconscious mind believes, and you definitely do not agree with it. At no point in the rest of the book do we assume you agree with *any* of these subconscious beliefs. Far from it. We take it as read that you *do not* agree with them.

Think of your mind as an iceberg. Your conscious mind is the little bit poking above the surface of the sea. That 5% contains all your conscious thoughts, desires, and beliefs about your worth, about equality, and all your understanding of the twenty-first century world. The

95% lurking beneath the surface contains something different. The set of beliefs, motivations and understandings down here is tangled, archaic, outdated, confused, fear-based, and has pretty much nothing to do with your present-day life. Unfortunately, these subconscious beliefs dominate the way we feel and subtly undermine us.

Your subconscious mind does not understand the twenty-first century. It is controlled by the archaic beliefs of the past, and it controls you without you realising it.

The Beast that lurks in your subconscious mind is not on your side. It doesn't want you to have happiness, freedom, opportunity and a fabulous career where you outshine all the men. That much is certain.

But this, again, is still only the beginning. Maybe you've done belief work before and used healing modalities to change your subconscious programmes. Doing this did improve things for me, but it didn't crack the real problem. Why? Because my subconscious was just the thin end of the wedge. The problem went deeper, into the energies of society itself and the power dynamics of human interaction. This was the true extent of The Beast.

For now, though, just realise that your subconscious mind is not your friend. It doesn't agree with you most of the time, and when it disagrees, it starts to sabotage and attack you in various and imaginative ways, to get you under control. When you feel blocked, stuck, held back by fears, your beast is doing its work.

Another way to look at this phenomenon is to think of your mind as a computer. Your conscious mind is your software. You choose the programmes you want to run; you're in control. Underneath the surface is your operating system. If your operating system is outdated, your software doesn't run well and conflicts cause your computer to crash. Your subconscious mind is your inherited operating system, and unfortunately, it is out of date and woefully inadequate if you're a modern, talented woman determined to flourish.

As we go through the book, I'll be flagging up the sabotaging subconscious patterns (our obsolete operating system) that I've seen in many, many women. Over the last two decades, I've spent thousands of hours identifying these specific belief patterns, and the same things come up again and again.

Please read the next paragraph at least twice.

These sabotaging belief patterns are programmed into our subconscious minds and our society at the energetic level, like old computer software. The words associated with these programmes will invariably sound archaic, extreme, violent, ridiculous even, to our twenty-first century selves, and bear no relation to our real world. Where I quote these programmes in the following chapters, I am using the words I have actually found to be present in my clients' subconscious minds over and over again.[3] This isn't wording that I've made up, or a sensible version that we think ought to be there, but the actual wording I have tested for and found to be present. It is the fact that these programmes are so extreme and so outdated, and yet hidden within us, that does so much damage.

As you read on, if you think something sounds ridiculous, don't dismiss it. Instead, ask yourself, 'If that programme is lurking in my subconscious mind, how will that undermine my confidence to do what I

---

3   Over two decades I have identified specific subconscious belief
     patterns in many people using a technique called muscle testing.
     This is similar to the techniques a kinesiologist applies to the body,
     but when focused on the mind it enables us to identify hidden
     programmes buried in the subconscious.

want in life?' or, 'If that belief is actually hidden in my subconscious mind, does that explain why my stress seems out of proportion?'

As we go on this journey together, I'll be introducing you to many of the negative and obsolete patterns which inhabit people's minds, the group consciousness and the energy matrix we all share. *This does not mean that the people in question consciously believe these things.* People usually believe the exact opposite in their conscious minds. However, it's the old, hidden energies lurking in our subconscious that we are concerned with. We all have them. There's no judgement attached here. This is simply the legacy we have inherited from the past.

A change in paradigm

The next leap I want you to take regards the nature of the world. The external, three-dimensional, solid world we all inhabit is simply the top layer of a deep energy structure. Despite the fact that quantum physics has shown all reality to be just a soup of probability, the old Newtonian solid physics still prevails in our minds. Don't worry, this isn't a book about physics, but if you are going to free yourself, you do need to think about the world in a different way.

Everything is energy. Everything is connected. Our thoughts, feelings and energy fields extend far beyond the limitations of our physical bodies. I expect you've heard this before. Well, I want you to consider now that you aren't living your life in isolation. Instead, you are plugged into the matrix of energy which makes up our world. Your mind and body are sensitive to the messages they receive from the surrounding energetic field, just as other people are sensitive to the messages you are putting out. We aren't separate; we are, indeed, connected. This means that you are constantly receiving a myriad of messages on many energetic levels as you go through your daily life and, unbeknownst to you, your mind and body are reacting to them.

In the rest of this book, we will be looking at the effect of this hidden energetic level on our responses and lives, and each time I use the word 'energetically', this hidden level is what I am referring to.

You are now ready to embark on your quest – your quest to vanquish The Beast and take your rightful place in the Palace of Success.

2
What Is Power?

Grace felt nervous, she was sure something was following her. She glanced over her shoulder again, and again, quickening her pace. Her heart began to race. 'Oh, don't be ridiculous,' she told herself. 'It's all in your imagination.' But this reminded her too much of the time when, as a little girl, she'd got lost on holiday. Ever since then, forests had freaked her out. Every rustle of the leaves, every crackle of sticks, made her jump.

By the time the wolf pounced, she was already a bundle of nerves. Grace shrieked, but being a competent girl, she seized a hefty stick and whacked the wolf soundly around the head. He certainly hadn't been expecting this response and beat a hasty retreat into the undergrowth. Severely shaken, Grace took to her heels and ran as fast as she possibly could. She no longer felt excited; she felt vulnerable. Every noise meant danger.

The ultimate humiliation

Let me share a story that still makes me feel physically sick just thinking about it. One day, back when I was a lecturer, I was invited by a well-regarded engineering company to carry out some collaborative experiments with them. I wrote a proposal and arrived to present it.

You know how this goes, the female receptionist was the first and last woman I saw. There we were in the meeting, myself and one of our technicians, with twelve industry men around this table. As the lead on the project, I was at the overhead projector explaining our proposal. Halfway through my presentation, one of the men interrupted with a question about the apparatus. I invited our technician to answer as appropriate, expecting to continue my presentation afterwards. That man then engaged the technician in a discussion, and just kept on talking. He brought other men around the table into the discussion. All the time I'm standing like a lemon at the overhead projector, waiting for them to shut up so I can continue with the presentation. You know what? They never did.

Can you believe, I stood there for an hour and a half, feeling as if I were inside the King's Palace with all my power stripped from me, suddenly invisible and irrelevant. I *desperately wanted* to say something. I *should have* called them to account and taken back control. But I just couldn't open my mouth. I literally couldn't do anything. I was utterly powerless in that situation.

I had gone into submission and was unable to get out. I was so humiliated by this experience that I didn't even tell anyone about it, not even my husband, for over twenty years.

Of course, this wasn't the only incident; it was one of many – some publicly humiliating like this one, and many others, more subtle. But with each, the same insidious message was repeated, over and over again. The message that I wasn't good enough, that I didn't have credibility, that I didn't command respect. This credibility and respect should have been mine automatically, given my qualifications and position, and certainly would have been, had I been male. And each time my reaction was the same: I let what little power I had drain away from me, leaving myself utterly vulnerable. When I look back and remember how it felt, it was as if I had been kept restrained in a straitjacket.

The power of human interaction

There are many different ways to look at power in human interaction. I use this one:

Power is the ability to create change.

We can hold legal rights and entitlements. We can have the ability and the desire, but if we can't *create* change we have no power. If we can't make things different, we can only react to the actions of others, and so they have the power.

When we have no power this triggers a survival instinct mechanism in our brains. When we have no power, our mind and body instantly feel in danger. All our stress and survival 'fight or flight' responses activate. I am no physiologist, but I have lived this response, over and over again. I have gone through this reaction so many times. It was my normal state of being for many years. I know for a fact that when I was in that downward spiral, my body was in that state pretty much all the time. There were times when I reckoned my blood was 90% adrenaline.

On the other hand, when we are able to effect change, our minds and bodies feel safe. Feeling safe is everything. Only then can the body relax; only then can the mind turn off the survival and stress responses that trigger all that anxiety.

If you're stuck in a cycle of stress and anxiety, depression or holding back, you can be sure your body knows you aren't in a position to create change. Here's the key fact – a fact that I didn't realise for a long time – this 'power' isn't a belief in your rights, it's an *energetic mechanism*.

As we go through life, there will be an ebb and flow of energy between people, but it's my experience that each person has a default state – either pulling energy in, which gives them power, or giving it away. When we are children, we simply observe the energy flow patterns we see around us and copy them. These patterns then define our interaction with the world.

This is the reason why conventional approaches to dealing with impostor syndrome, stress and lack of confidence fall at the first hurdle. We can change our conscious thoughts; we can release limiting beliefs; we can train ourselves to use assertive body language, but that still doesn't give us the power that we need to feel safe and thrive. We have to correct the flow of energy to have power, and all the conventional approaches fail to do this.

Our evolutionary handicap: submission

Here's the bottom line: women are hardwired to give their power away – to go into submission. This means letting energy flow away from us, leaving us powerless. I know this sounds controversial, but bear with me and let me explain.

Think back to the start of human society: a world based purely on survival. In such a world, the strong would prevail and the weak would submit. In such a society, any man who wanted a woman would just take her. The stronger tribe would seize the land of the weaker. Physical strength was the law. In such a society, physically weak individuals would submit to the strong to avoid being destroyed and to seek protection. We see this response everywhere in the animal kingdom. The weaker animal exposes its vulnerable throat and belly to the alpha, and this submission defines the hierarchy of the group. Not only that, if those animals had been fighting for dominance, in that moment of submission, the beaten animal gives away all its power. On a deep energetic level, this dynamic became locked into a patriarchal society. We may like to think of ourselves as civilised and above such basic reactions, but the truth is these drivers are still in play every day, for everyone, with the veneer of our modern world simply plastered over the top.

For so long, I tried to train myself to feel confident and empowered when I interacted with people, and I failed. Eventually, I understood what was happening. What I was doing with my conscious mind was completely irrelevant, because my body was going into submission. My body was perceiving my world as full of danger, everyone around me as a genuine threat to my life. This instinctual reaction was triggering, and I submitted on the energetic level. When I did this, I gave away all my power to the other person. This had nothing to do with my conscious understanding of my safety, rights, abilities, and the law. No, it was an automatic response programmed deep in my mind and body, which simply activated again, and again, and again.

Regardless of our conscious desires and aspirations, our subconscious mind and body are playing the old game of submission. This automatic response drains our power and keeps us at a perpetual energetic disadvantage. It's no wonder we hold back.

When I realised this, everything became clear and the picture that had eluded me for so long began to fall into place. With this awareness, I became increasingly sensitive to the dynamics of what I was doing, and I began analysing my responses meticulously. I would feel fairly strong by myself, then, as soon as I had to interact with someone, I felt my power draining away, leaving me unable to do anything more than react – regardless of how hard my conscious mind was trying to make me assert myself. I discovered the alarming truth that I was living my life in submission. What is more, the feeling was so familiar that I realised I had been doing this my whole life.

As soon as we go into submission, the survival part of our brain starts to panic. We no longer have power, we can't create change, we aren't safe. This triggers all the stress responses I had struggled with all my life: anxiety, fear, panic, inability to speak up... the works.

I had a new understanding of my reaction, but a huge question remained: why did normal life, where there were no ferocious bears, mad axemen, impending executions or monsters, have this effect on me? Why was it that my body perceived the world I was inhabiting as cause to go into complete and utter submission?

Here are the facts I had to work with.

I was living in a free country, at a time when women officially had equal rights. I was highly qualified and hard-working, and entirely capable of doing the job I had been employed to do. I was not doing anything criminal. I was living in a country without major tornados, earthquakes or volcanoes. In a nutshell, I should have felt pretty safe. Certainly, I should have felt safe getting up, going to work, teaching my students, interacting with my colleagues and coming home again. On the surface, I was extremely good at my job. I could give a lecture to a couple of hundred students confidently and competently, publish high-quality scientific papers in peer-reviewed journals, and speak at international conferences. On the surface, all appeared fine. Yet underneath the picture was completely different. Something about my everyday life was triggering an extreme response in me, which my brain equated to life-threatening danger.

It doesn't take a PhD to see that these things simply do not add up. Something was missing from the equation. Discovering what that was would unlock the solution.

How submissive are you?

It's now time for you to use this new understanding to start analysing your own life, and the first essential step is to look at how often you are functioning with little or no power.

I know that the whole concept of submission will be positively abhorrent to a twenty-first century woman such as yourself. I'm sure you resist it with every fibre of your being. However, bear with me and let's investigate this scientifically.

Fact one: when you are holding your power, your mind and body will feel energetically safe and this leads naturally to feelings of confidence, wellbeing and flow.

Fact two: when you have gone into submission, you have zero power. This triggers all the instinctual reactions to being in danger and a cascade of stress responses in your body. It's then a case of fight or flight.

Fact three: this submission is an energetic response over which you have no conscious control. It is happening under the surface while consciously you are pushing yourself to be assertive, be confident, promote yourself, speak up, embrace your rights etc. It is this *conflict* that creates the problems.

If you were consciously submissive, you wouldn't be reading this book!

EXERCISE: WHERE ARE YOU GOING INTO SUBMISSION?

Part A: How do you feel in the below situations? Is flight your submission response?

Note that you can perform brilliantly and still experience these feelings under the surface, as I did. It is how you feel inside that we are interested in here. Consider how you feel when:

1. Speaking to people you don't know
2. Making phone calls
3. Speaking up in social gatherings or work meetings
4. Disagreeing with people
5. Doing a presentation or giving a performance
6. Travelling to new places alone

7. Discussing money – salary, promotion, fees from clients, making an offer for your services etc

8. Giving negative feedback to people in a work situation, or telling someone off

9. Expressing a strong opinion on a controversial subject where you know people will disagree with you

10. Being in a situation where there is confrontation, raised voices or aggression of any kind

11. Receiving criticism, both personal and professional

12. Receiving a critical, or downright nasty comment on one of your social media posts

Consider these situations in your professional life, your home life, and your intimate relationships, as your reactions can be different in different areas of your life. For each of these situations, critically analyse whether or not you feel relaxed, confident and at ease with being noticed, able to express yourself, competent and able to deal with the situation? Alternatively, do these situations trigger a pang of anxiety in your stomach, feelings of stress, worry and fear? Do they make you agonise and over-analyse? If so, you are going into energetic submission, and flight is your way of surviving.

Part B: The aggression submission response – is fight your submission response?

Another way to react when you go into energetic submission is anger and aggression. This may make you feel powerful on the surface and indeed will often get you what you want, but under the surface, you are still weak and, over time, this response will undermine you. To see whether this applies to you, answer the following:

1. Do you need anger or to 'fight' to get things done?

2. Do you lash out at other people?

3. Do you lose control in any way when coming up against resistance from others?

4. Do you post angry messages on social media to make you feel strong or justified, and feel the need to swear to make your point?

5. Do you find it hard to let go of resentments and grudges?

6. Do you enjoy getting into arguments on social media?

7. Are you energised by confrontation?

If you recognise yourself here, then any situation that triggered these responses has caused you to go into energetic submission and you have compensated by taking on a surface-level attacking stance. This may work as a facilitating mechanism, but it is not true power or strength. It is force without true power. You are still submitting at an energetic level, but fight is your response.

Part C: How much of your life is sabotaged by submission at the energetic level?

1. What proportion of your personal life triggers you to respond with submission?

2. What proportion of your professional life triggers you to respond with submission?

3. Overall, are you spending a significant proportion of your life in submission?

What did you find? How much of your life is controlled by your going into submission? Most women are surprised by how much of their life they are moving through without any true energetic power.

Remember, there is no judgement here. Denial achieves nothing. Clarity gives you a way forward, to change things. Acknowledging where in life you are giving away your power is the first step to reclaiming it.

3
Feminine Wounds

Grace came from a long line of women with magical powers. Truth be told, she had the heritage of a sorceress, like every woman before her and after her. As a child, she'd often used her magical powers to make things better, prettier or more fun. She'd written in 'fairy language' and changed the world with her mind.

Then she'd gone to school and everything had changed. 'Your powers aren't allowed,' the teacher had said. 'If you use them, you'll be punished.' So, over the years, Grace had forgotten she had magical powers at all.

The gender qualities of power

The women who get stuck in an automatic submission response have feminine wounds frozen in their past. To understand what I mean by this, you first need to know that power can have either a male or female quality. Male and female power are intrinsically different and all people, both men and women, will have a combination of the two. While some people have an equal balance of power, in my experience, most will be either female or male power dominant. (Think of it as the power version of yin and yang.)

Depending upon our life experience and the situation, our power can be either flowing or wounded. When we feel safe, our power will be at its best and will be of benefit to everyone. On the other hand, when we feel threatened, traumatised, crushed or otherwise triggered, our power becomes wounded, and either its character warps or it shuts down altogether.

When male power is flowing, it is goal-orientated, strong, supportive, active, focused, analytical – and useful for moving sofas. When male power is wounded, it becomes domineering, aggressive, confrontational, sometimes violent, controlling, violating and egotistical.

Let's make something clear. *It's not only men who can have wounded male power. A woman who is male power dominant can also have wounded male power, and consequently interact with those aggressive qualities.* I'm using the word 'male' to describe the *nature* of the wounded power, *not* the *gender* of the person wielding that power. Got it?

When female power is flowing, it is caring, loving, compassionate, intuitive, gentle, imaginative, receptive and nurturing. It contains all that Earth Mother strength: the courage of the mother bear protecting her cubs, the resilience of the woman starving herself so her children can eat, the determination of the suffragette fighting for what is right.

There is a big problem, though: if you are female power dominant, and are exposed to wounded male power, this has a specific negative effect. You will shut down your power centres and freeze in a wounded state; this is what I call a feminine wound. In this wounded state, your true power is effectively neutralised and this has profound repercussions that affect how you react and cope with life from that point onwards. I'll be dealing with how to free yourself from this in detail, later in the book.

Many women are not living with healthy female power at all, and are instead living with permanently wounded power. Many of us don't even know what flowing female power feels like. This leads to the common misconception that female power is weak. It's not. We've just confused our true power with the wounded version. Unfortunately, the more wounding we suffer, the further away we are taken from our true power, and the more locked into submission we become. It's a vicious cycle.

What causes feminine wounds?

What sort of experiences cause feminine wounds? The cycle starts with anything which, rightly or wrongly, makes your subconscious believe you are in danger. These incidents start in childhood and can be big or small, one-off or chronic. An incident can be genuine danger, or it can be your child's mind completely misunderstanding what is going on. It can start with something as simple as being told off, witnessing adults arguing or a teacher shouting at the class. If you were exposed to any sort of abuse (mental, emotional, sexual or physical) at any age, or suffered any kind of violence, this will certainly have caused feminine wounds. If you were bullied, verbally put down or constantly ignored, these will have had a similar effect. You will have collected feminine wounds even if you had a happy, nurturing childhood. We all have them. The opportunities to be wounded are endless.

This is how it works. The first wounding probably happens early in childhood. Your mind registers danger and, as a small girl, your instinctual response is to go into submission and give your power away. Part of you stays frozen in that experience and labels everything associated with it as dangerous. Your subconscious creates extreme programmes such as 'I'm going to die' or 'I'm not allowed to exist', links them with the experience and locks the whole thing in place, on the energetic level. The automatic subconscious response has now been set up.

The next time something similar happens, this automatic response is triggered and, before you know it, anxiety, fear and panic are coursing through your veins, whether or not the situation warrants this reaction. Think of it as an energetic knee-jerk response to life. You don't have time to analyse, discern or decide whether there is a real threat or not. Your system simply goes into autopilot.

To compound things, each wounding experience has a cumulative effect, reinforcing the message that the world is dangerous. Before you know where you are, you've reached adulthood saddled with a catalogue of frozen experiences. Each locks you more firmly into submission and defines your power response for the rest of your life. Your true power has been shut down, and your default response is now to assume danger and react with submission on the energetic level.

Why doesn't your subconscious mind update itself and come to see the difference between true danger and something else? Why doesn't it realise that you're a grown woman and not a defenceless little girl? Why doesn't it understand that the originally perceived danger is long gone, or indeed never really existed at all?

These are good questions. Alas, my decades of experience working with feminine wounds have taught me that they never heal spontaneously. This is why we get stuck in patterns of disempowerment that can last a lifetime. The extent to which all this affects you will depend upon your character, your actual experiences, and some other factors that we'll get to in a moment. For now, all you need to understand is that feminine wounding will have fundamentally sabotaged your empowerment.

Living with your power shut down

You need power to survive and function in life, and yet your power has been shut down. So, what do you do next? At this point, there are two ways you can go. Either you shut down altogether and live your life like a mouse, hardly making an impact on anyone or anything (as you are reading this book, it is unlikely that you have gone this way). Or, you adopt a coping strategy to compensate for your wounded power. This coping strategy, usually created in childhood, becomes your permanent, automatic response to life and holds you back as an adult. Unfortunately, reacting in this way will never support your success, happiness and achievement in the long-term, because it is a fear-based survival response.

There are several compensation mechanisms that women typically adopt, and you'll learn about these and identify how you have been coping on the energetic level in the chapter on Female Power Archetypes. For now, understand that you have been going through life with an enormous power handicap.

Your instinctual submission response, compounded by your feminine wounds, has left you running on empty. That you're functioning at all is, frankly, a miracle. If you've already achieved things in your life, that's pretty amazing.

CLIENT STORY: AYESHA[4]

When Ayesha came to me she was a successful business coach and, on the surface at least, had things together. However, she confided that she had real problems with anxiety, struggled to speak up, suffered from impostor syndrome (feeling deep down that she was a fraud), and the resulting stress was beginning to affect her health. She had been diagnosed with chronic fatigue syndrome (just as I had, years previously) and felt herself spiralling into a pattern of burnout.

Being an expert in her branch of personal development, she was very much an awakened woman and had done a great deal of work on herself. She had received healing and coaching from the best and had already released a lot of sabotaging conditioning from her life. She couldn't understand why she was still struggling with these patterns.

When we began to look at her past, the reason became clear. She had faced two big challenges in her childhood. She was from a very traditional patriarchal family in which girls were not given the freedom or opportunities showered upon the boys. This constant messaging of 'you are inferior to the boys' and 'your

---

4   I have changed names to protect the identities of my clients in the stories I have shared.

place is to serve the men' had undermined her on so many levels and caused many feminine wounds.

In addition, her mother, now deceased, had suffered from mental illness, which had resulted in trauma and violence during Ayesha's early years. This had naturally made her feel unsafe at the deepest level. She had received a lot of counselling, but I knew full well that the worst experiences would still be frozen within her, and while they stayed this way, she would always be locked in those moments of fear and submission. These experiences would have one of two possible effects on her. Either she would be crushed, or she would compensate and strive to prove herself despite what she had been through.

Ayesha was a high-achieving woman who had gone on to succeed in the world by anyone's standards – clearly, she had taken the path of proving herself. The trouble was that, as an independent professional woman, her life was totally at odds with her subconscious programming about what she needed to do to be safe. The resulting inner conflict was creating the anxiety and burnout she was experiencing.

Obviously, in Ayesha's case, there wasn't just one big incident to clear, but many, accumulated over several years. With the right energetic tools, I was able to bring her out of those experiences, reclaim her power from her family in those memories and shift the balance of power back to her. When those events were unfrozen, her energetic power returned. We could then start the process of changing her conditioning. As expected, this proved to be the key to her recovery.

Those experiences that upset or frightened you, big and small, created sabotaging patterns of submission and accompanying subconscious programmes of fear. No matter how much counselling or healing you have received, how much personal development you've gone through, and how much you believe you have put these events behind you and moved on, until you get your power back and redefine your automatic responses, your feminine wounds will continue to define your life.

Sometimes women are astounded at just how trivial these frozen experiences turn out to be – incidents they'd completely forgotten about. All it takes is a knee-jerk fear response at the time, especially during childhood, to set up sabotaging patterns that can have far-reaching consequences.

Identifying our wounds, unfreezing them and reclaiming our power at the energetic level, is the key to shifting our power response to life.

4

Forbidden

Grace looked at the chasm she had to cross and the bottom dropped out of her stomach. Stretching across the gulf was a rope bridge, the sort of thing you'd find in the rainforest. Tentatively, she began to inch her way across, clinging on for dear life. The bridge swayed alarmingly beneath her. Her head was spinning, she felt sick. How was she ever going to make it to the other side?

Across the valley, she could see George striding confidently across his sturdy stone bridge. 'Hurry up, Grace,' he cried jovially. 'You're taking ages.' 'Good grief,' she thought to herself. 'Can't he see I'm suspended above nothing here?'

Your missing power foundation

The key understanding that has been missing from all female empowerment up until now, is that of power foundation. This is something we feel in our lives – or, more accurately, feel the lack of. Let me explain.

The power foundation is the energetic support that gives us our entitlement and our ability to create and use our power in the world. Having a power foundation makes us feel safe and confident. Without it, we feel unsafe and unsupported. Without a power foundation, we will always struggle to create in the world, because there is nothing beneath us.

Let's start by considering what a man feels when he goes out to make his way in the world, taking George as our example. Let's say George graduates from university and goes to work for a big company, where he rises to the level of Executive. He earns an excellent salary. He commands respect and has status at work and in his community. How supported and entitled is he going to feel in his position? The answer is, very. The conditioning he experienced throughout his childhood, historical precedents and the law of the land for centuries all establish his birthright to command, to have a high-status job, to earn that salary and to lead. These things are not only ingrained in his subconscious mind but are essentially imprinted into every cell in his body. There's no way he would feel he's doing something forbidden or dangerous. There is no way he'd feel that he's going against his ancestry, the law and precedent. He has a strong power foundation. He has a huge energetic advantage given to him, as a man, by history.

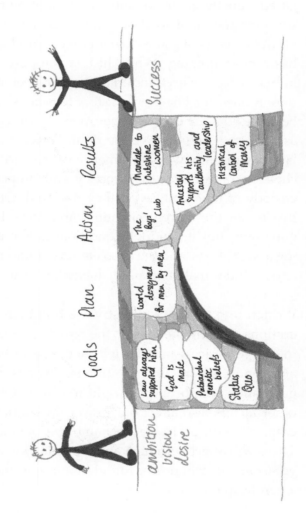

WHAT MEN EXPERIENCE

Goals   Plan   Action   Results

ambition
vision
desire

Law always supported him
God is male
Patriarchal gender beliefs
Status Quo

world designed for men by men

The Boys' Club

Mandate to Outshine women

Ancestry supports his authority and leadership

Historical control of Money

Success

A man's path to success is secure and assured because of his firm power foundation. It's like a sturdy stone bridge to his destination.

What about a woman's power foundation? Say Grace decides on a similar career to George. She is equally gifted, equally qualified, and twenty-first century law supports her right to choose any career she wishes. However, when it comes to her power foundation, she has almost nothing. While history supports George in his choices, everything that has come before Grace undermines her. For Grace, history tells her she should be in the home, she should obey men, she isn't as clever as men, she doesn't have the right. For centuries, the law has disempowered women with respect to their choices, control over their money and property, and custody of their children if they divorced. Of course, this is not the current situation, and these laws are gone now, but the hidden conditioning, the underlying assumptions, and the obsolete subconscious beliefs and attitudes that affect us all, haven't yet caught up.

Written into George's ancestry are hundreds of generations of being the master, the breadwinner, the one in charge. Grace's ancestry tells her she is subservient and cannot be any of those things. She has only one generation supporting her right to power. Of course, other factors also affect our power foundation: class, caste, religion and race, to name the obvious ones. These will affect both men and women. However, the *gender disparity* in power foundation is enormous and a handicap that all women have.

Over the course of the twentieth century, there was a phenomenal change in women's rights and freedoms – and not before time. Here's the problem, though: we now have the freedom to do what we want, achieve outside the home, and outshine men, but we only have this in the conscious, visible world. The subconscious world, and the legacy energies that surround us, have not caught up. The old energetic structures lag behind and we feel them undermining us.

A quick way of assessing how far your subconscious mind is lagging behind your actual rights is to consider your immediate reaction to the following list of professions. Say each word to yourself. In how many cases does your mind automatically picture that person as a man?

Here's the list:

Banker, scientist, chief executive, actuary, professor, vice-chancellor, consultant, judge, engineer, chef, chief financial officer, IT consultant, astronaut, police superintendent, entrepreneur, surgeon.

When I do this exercise, I am appalled that my subconscious mind will still assume a man first, even for professions that I have had myself: scientist, engineer, university lecturer. When I do this with my students and clients, without exception the result is the same. Despite being modern women, our subconscious minds are still on a different page: the page of the past.

This knee-jerk reaction demonstrates that the male entitlement energy prevails and female entitlement energy is simply not yet there. Subconsciously, it is still a surprise for a woman to have one of these jobs. This phenomenon exists in every man's mind, too. Every woman who chooses to be and do something beyond the domestic world is up against this lack of power foundation.

The 'kitchen maid to university-made' timeline

The best way to understand and measure your lack of power foundation, and how it can affect you, is to look at the last couple of generations in your family. Look at what your mother, grandmother, and maybe great grandmother had in terms of choice, opportunity, education, aspiration and freedom.

If I look at this pattern within my own family, the red flags are clear. My maternal grandmother, Lily, a caring and courageous lady, started out as a kitchen maid and later became a cook. My mother, Ruth, received her education during the transition years, when opportunities were opening up for women. She was able to go to teacher training college from school, then twenty years later went to university and got her BA degree. In contrast, I went to Cambridge straight from school and have a first-class science degree and a PhD. The aspirations and opportunities that I have had are light years away from my grandmother's, in the space of just two generations.

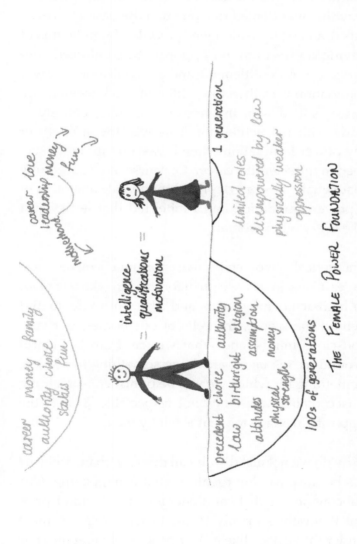

career   money   family
authority   choice
status   fun

intelligence
= qualifications =
motivation

career   love
leadership money
motherhood   fun

precedent   choice   authority
law   birthright   religion
attitudes   assumption
physical   money
strength

limited roles
disempowered by law
physically weaker
oppression

100s of generations

1 generation

THE FEMALE POWER FOUNDATION

The female power foundation is practically non-existence. No matter how equal we are on the surface, in terms of qualifications and opportunity, the foundation we have inherited is one of disempowerment.

The rapid shift in women's rights during the twentieth century gave me the freedom to develop my gifts in a way that was denied to women in the past. However, this dramatic transition was preceded by millennia of having no freedom, no opportunities, enforced subservience, no entitlement and no choice. My power foundation was, therefore, still that of a kitchen maid. It was still that of my female ancestors, entirely at odds with my actual life. This was the strength of my power foundation when I was attempting to succeed in my scientific career. Of course, it was woefully inadequate. History deprived my female ancestors of a power foundation and I inherited that legacy, just like every other woman.

Energetically, women receive enormously mixed messages. Consciously, we push forward to take our place in high-achieving careers and are right to do so. But behind the scenes, the cells of our bodies, our subconscious minds, and what we feel from the world around us, tell us we are doing something forbidden. Something for which we will be punished, something unacceptable, unseemly, not respectable. This is the opposite message to what is felt by men.

Why do we not just dismiss all this as archaic rubbish? It's because we don't realise what is happening. Our subconscious beliefs and energetic labels don't present themselves openly to us. Instead, they sit there under the surface like a slow poison, seeping into our lives, undermining our resolve and pulling the rug out from under us day after day.

The forbidden labels

It's important at this point to understand how our minds and bodies decide, overall, if we are safe and entitled to be somewhere and do something. You probably assume that you make these decisions just by looking at the facts. As a general rule, men do this. Women, on the other hand, are far more likely to be influenced by the subtle energies around us, and our minds and bodies will be hugely influenced by what we feel, by the undercurrents and the subtle signals we pick up from people and institutions. These subtle energies usually dominate for us, and actually define our response.

Here lies our big problem. Women's history has essentially put an energetic label of 'forbidden' on everything outside the traditional realm of the home. Probably the only careers not forbidden are cleaner and midwife! Every step we take outside those limits invites the message 'This is forbidden for a woman'. These energetic labels are not only picked up by us, but also held in the subconscious minds of everyone around us. This means that, despite the facts, what we *feel* is zero energetic entitlement to be high-achieving women. We *feel* zero energetic entitlement to outshine men, zero energetic entitlement to be in authority.

The fact that we legally have these rights simply isn't enough to make our bodies and our subconscious minds feel that we are entitled, because they are being bombarded with contradictory energetic messages. Without entitlement, we don't feel safe. Without safety, we go into energetic submission.

Look no further for the true root of unconscious bias against women. Here is another important equation:

$$\text{Subconscious 'forbidden' labels} + \text{No power foundation} = \text{Unconscious bias}$$

To show you how universal this subconscious labelling problem is, here are some numbers. Of the fifty-seven women I have worked with on a one-to-one basis for stress, anxiety, confidence issues and impostor syndrome over the last few years (including accountants, academics, coaches, healers, medics, entrepreneurs, a 'red carpet' actress, burlesque dancers, a mathematician, a filmmaker, and lawyers) a staggering 100% had the subconscious belief that what they were doing was forbidden. Yes, 100%. What is more, 95% of them also had the subconscious programming that they would be punished for breaking the 'law' by having these careers, and 82% had the programming that they would be put to death. Their subconscious programming had not updated to the twenty-first century, and they were fighting against it every single day, just as I had been. Needless to say, all these women were astonished and appalled when they discovered such beliefs were there under the surface of their minds.

I am a great example that proves how much the subconscious mind dominates. My parents gave me and my brother equal opportunities and encouraged me to take on a traditionally male career, as did my school. My childhood should have set me up for success in that realm, but it didn't.

When I tested my own subconscious programming years later, I discovered that my mind held the obsolete programmes that going to university was forbidden for a woman; doing a PhD was forbidden; being a university lecturer and scientist was forbidden; having authority over my students (the majority of whom were male, of course) was forbidden; being on an equal level with my male colleagues was forbidden; outshining men in anything was forbidden. My whole life was subconsciously labelled as forbidden, despite the obvious opportunities and freedom I'd had.

Consciously, I believed I was the equal of all the men and was determined to succeed and outshine them wherever possible. Although I had no concept of my missing power foundation, I felt that lack of energetic support. Looking back, I felt like Grace crossing the chasm. I had nothing under me. I felt unsafe. I was doing something wrong. I walked into that engineering department and felt one big 'No!' It's no wonder my mind and body interpreted my situation as dangerous and began to trigger submission, anxiety and the cascade of power-deficit reactions that we women show so frequently.

CLIENT STORY: PAULINE

When Pauline walked into my healing room, I could have been looking back in time and seeing myself thirty years ago. She was an undergraduate at a top university, just as I had been. Despite her obvious intelligence and motivation, she had been struck down with panic attacks, insomnia, anxiety, and pretty much everything that had started my own spiral downward. She had reached the point of self-harm. Her college had been supportive, giving her time out to try and recover before continuing with her degree, but this wasn't making any difference to the way she felt.

On the day we met, she was in a bad way. She had only been managing a couple of hours' sleep a night. She was tense and anxious, and looked crushed. Hers was a typical case of the high-achieving young woman going into institutions where everything is subconsciously labelled as forbidden. A bit of testing and we established that her subconscious programming forbade her from living away from home before she was married; forbade her from going to university; forbade her from getting an education; forbade her from having a job at all, let alone a high-powered career. We took a look at the underlying energies of her college, and although it had been admitting women for several years, the energetic message of its group consciousness was still 'men only'.

Pauline was feeling the double whammy of her ancestral programming, which told her what she was doing was utterly forbidden, and then going into an environment that carried the same energetic message. Even though the college authorities were supportive and committed to equal opportunities, the underlying energetic structure wasn't aligned with this reality and was instead stuck in the past.

Being a sensitive woman, Pauline had felt both the obsolete energies of the institution and of her ancestral programming and reacted to that messaging without knowing what it was. Naturally, her subconscious mind had gone into meltdown and believed she would be punished for the 'crime' of unacceptable female behaviour. I know this extreme programming sounds ridiculous in light of the reality, but trust me, I've found these things time and time again.

As predicted, when we had removed those obsolete forbidden labels from her mind's operating system and I had taught her how to bring back her power on the energetic level, she was able to return to college and did excellently in her exams.

Modern women are usually shocked when they find out just how weak their power foundation is. When I bring up this concept, they often express resistance and denial. This is especially true for those who are warrior types. However, knowledge is the first step to genuine power, and it serves no purpose to avoid looking at what is essentially a weak link in your life. The weaker your foundation, the more your success and wellbeing will be undermined and blocked, so it's important to realise the truth of your situation.

You'll be analysing your power foundation later on in the book. For now, let me leave you with this thought. If you have achieved any degree of success before now, without a strong power foundation, how much more could you achieve when you correct this? This is the missing link you've been waiting for.

5
Perfection Is Male

George and Grace stood together in the castle grounds. The contest was about to begin. Grace read the long list of rules in her hand.

'Rules for men: Be a leader. Be strong. Be assertive. Be authoritative. Take the initiative. Give commands. Be confident. Promote yourself. Succeed. This makes you a proper man.

Rules for women: Be demure, modest and only speak when spoken to. Keep your eyes downcast. Never leave the house. Don't show your intelligence. Put yourself down. Don't assert yourself. Put everyone else's needs before your own. Sacrifice your success to make sure others succeed. Avoid the spotlight. Never answer back. Wear a corset. And above all, never outshine a man, even if he's a total imbecile. This makes you a proper woman.

We pride ourselves on our equal opportunities policy. Women are permitted to enter the contest, as long as they obey the above rules.'

'Excellent,' said George. 'I forbid you from beating me.'

'What the * &ˆˇ % & * $!?' Grace spluttered.

Classical perfection

All you have to do is look to Michelangelo's famous image of God giving life to Adam – in fact, I use this image when I am teaching where the idea of 'perfection' comes from. The male God gives the male Adam life – perfection is male.

It was while studying art history A Level – a bit odd for a scientist, I know, but it kept me sane – that I had a revelation. I loved the journey deep into the world of the Italian Renaissance. Hour after hour I spent in a little room in the art department with an old-fashioned slide projector, studying the masters: Botticelli, Piero Della Francesca, Titian, Leonardo Da Vinci and, of course, Michelangelo. For months, it all washed over me as I absorbed perspective and proportion, and the classical ideal of beauty in form. It was fascinating to me and I loved it, until the day my inspiring art teacher, Miss Date, talked about the 'Golden Section' and showed the ratio clearly marked in Leonardo da Vinci's Vitruvian Man (circa 1490) – the perfect ratio on the perfect male body.

I had a sudden moment of clarity – this 'ideal beauty' of the human body being shown was male. The more I thought about it, the more I realised that *all* the messages of perfection we were being shown were male.

The full understanding didn't come until I did the work that I teach today, but I look back at that moment and see what lay at the root of it all. No matter what I did, I would always be me. I could not be what the world labelled 'perfect', and neither could any woman. This is what the whole Classical world, the Renaissance, right up to our modern Western civilisation, has told us. Back in that art room, I didn't understand how significant this was, but it is the key to everything. Our world was created by men, in their image, to suit them: their attributes, bodies, characteristics, ways of doing things and ideals. They were set as the gold standard, the perfect way, the only way.

The subconscious message for us women is, 'I'm female; therefore, my body is imperfect. I'm not good enough. No matter how hard I try, no matter what I achieve and how many men I outshine with my brilliance, I cannot be perfect. Ever.' All this is then exacerbated by cultural taboos around the female reproductive system and sex, which label us as unclean. Men are perfect, and we are sullied; there isn't much equality there. This 'male is perfect' energy is deeply ingrained in all our institutions, our attitudes, and our world, and we, as women, feel it under the surface. This is at the core of what undermines our confidence, our female power and our success. This is the true root of our struggles with impostor syndrome and feeling not good enough.

A world made by men, to suit men

Now let's take our understanding to the next level. Bearing in mind that we are starting out locked into submission mode, fighting against those 'forbidden' labels, with zero power foundation, we are already at a disadvantage.

The default human is male – this is the belief that ultimately disempowers women. The world was designed by men, for men, and 'man' is the shape of perfection. No matter where we go, this message is there in our faces, ingrained on so many levels.

Everything we aspire to has been created as a male version. This sends us the perpetual subconscious message that we aren't allowed. Would you go into the gents' toilet?

This issue has many more dimensions than the visible manifestations, but let's start with those. At the top, those trivial things that we aren't supposed to make a fuss about, like 'he' being used as the default pronoun. There are so many examples: phones that are too big to hold; high stools that are incompatible with skirts; regulatory car safety tests using fiftieth-percentile male crash-test dummies to represent the whole adult population; the International Space Station having only one working medium-sized space suit, delaying the first all-female spacewalk. I don't intend to go into data analysis here, but highly recommend Caroline Criado Perez's award-winning book *Invisible Women: Exposing data bias in a world designed for men*, which brilliantly analyses the extent of this problem. You can read the appalling facts for yourself there.

But let's go deeper. The typical work environment, culture, way of behaving – my own experience was that this was the wounded male way. Confrontational, competitive and, in many instances, back-stabbing and aggressive. Admittedly, my work environment was an extreme example, being in such a male-dominated discipline, but even if you have chosen a career where women are properly represented, the culture, the energetic structures will, in nearly all cases, be male-based because of the inherited legacy.

If I look at my way of interacting with people, I find I'm gentle, supportive, I see concepts as beautiful and elegant. I like to feel things and allow my intuition to contribute to my work. Although I have an analytical and logical scientific brain, when it comes to my way of living and interacting with others, I'm very female. When I attempted to be that woman, to be my true self, in my workplace, I may as well have been speaking Greek. At best, I was ignored; at worst I was put down, crushed, laughed at. The lesson was clear on so many levels. If I wanted to survive, I was expected to be like them. But of course, I couldn't be like them, because that wasn't me and never could be.

How many of us female achievers struggle with perfectionism and not feeling good enough? Here we find the root of the problem. Already undermined by our submission response, which takes away our power, we are then shown the default energetic level expectations of our world. Perfection is male. What can we do with this? On the energetic level, the world expects us to be something we can never be. So the rug is pulled out from under our self-esteem.

Impostor syndrome? We *are* impostors. We are women who are trying to succeed in a world where men are still the benchmark. We are conditioned by our lack of power foundation; conditioned by history; conditioned by many generations of precedent; conditioned by the subconscious energies of the people and institutions around us. The rules we perceive in our minds and bodies tell us our way is not acceptable. Our bodies are the wrong shape. We operate in the wrong way. We think in the wrong way. The things we need to thrive are forbidden. Our female powers are forbidden.

The 'God is male' justification

Exacerbating the social legacy, we have the added validation from religion. Yes, that old chestnut. Nearly all the major religions are patriarchal. Whether or not you are religious, your ancestors would have been, and those beliefs are deeply ingrained into our cultural DNA, the group consciousness, family patterning and our individual subconscious minds. There are so many religious messages labelling the male as superior, more spiritual, closer to God. So many messages telling women we are unclean and inferior. There is enough material here for at least another three books. Suffice it to say, our religious heritage puts male divinity firmly at the top of the hierarchy, endowing men with authority over women. What better way to entrench our subservience and obedience?

While I know you don't consciously believe these things, I also know that the programming of your subconscious mind will be deeply influenced by old religious justifications for men keeping us oppressed. This adds a deeper, fear-based control to those forbidden labels. They are often linked, deep in our subconscious minds, with a concept of divine retribution that our ancestors believed in. I know it

sounds extreme, but I have found these blocks countless times.

The patriarchy box

There is only one thing we can do. We can shut down
all the parts of ourselves that are 'unacceptable', and
try to make ourselves fit the compulsory energetic
mould. But which set of parameters do we use? There
are two. The parameters of success, which are male and
don't fit us, and those old historical parameters of what
a woman should be (quiet, demure obedient, etc). The
result? You'll know exactly what the result is, because
you are most likely living it. That result is inner conflict.

This is the hidden battle you are fighting every day.
Without your power, your body is stuck in submission, a terrified state as its baseline. Everything you
want to do is labelled as forbidden. Everything about
you is unacceptable because perfection is male. To try
and conform, you shut down more parts of yourself
– the parts that are your unique female spark – and
you become even less whole. Your mind and body feel
even more powerless.

The bottom line: we are constrained from all directions. Everything in the world stops us from fully
activating our unique female power. The legacy we
are up against undermines us at every turn. It's a

non-resolving loop. A conundrum we cannot solve. We are stuck between the proverbial rock and a hard place.

Can you imagine the quagmire of conflicting beliefs, rules, and energies we are struggling against? None of them supports our freedom, our right to be and do exactly what we want with our lives. Our internal conflict is off the scale.

If this is where you find yourself, you are probably coping to a certain level. You might be able to go on for years before the cracks start to show; or, you might start to fall apart almost immediately. I have seen both. One thing is always true: when a woman shuts down who she really is, and tries to squeeze herself into the patriarchy box, there is always a cost. Maybe the cost is your relationship, your happiness, your success, your health, your wellbeing – or all of these. The cost is huge and we shouldn't have to pay it.

While you are suppressing your natural way of being and thinking, you dull your light, crush your confidence and ultimately undermine your wellbeing. The more you try to squeeze yourself into a box that doesn't fit, the more you will feel that you are not good enough, and the more likely you are to fall into the trap of destructive perfectionism and impostor syndrome.

One size doesn't fit all

In 1998 I was lecturing second-year materials science to mechanical engineers. One of the few female students came up to me after the lecture and was clearly upset. She had been handed an anonymous note during the lecture which told her she shouldn't be there because she didn't have the correct genitals (in less polite language). You can imagine how angry I was. I realised that there was no specific support set up within the department for our minority of female students, and I flagged this up with the authorities, suggesting that we needed a designated female tutor for female students – someone with a woman's understanding. I was told that support specifically for females would be against the rules because all students had to be treated the same. The university abided by a strict equal opportunities policy, but in this instance, it backfired. It is not possible to equate the needs of a man, sitting in a majority of 95%, in a male-friendly environment, with the needs of a female student, in a minority of 5%, in an environment unfriendly to females. Her experience will always be entirely different.

The university, while following its strict equal opportunities policy, was inadvertently failing to recognise the added challenges that minority female students faced. Additional support was, in my opinion, needed to level the playing field and enable them to truly be given an equal opportunity.

This was just one incident, but I've met the same sort of thing over and over again. In adopting a 'one size fits all' approach, the world invariably sets that size as 'male' –and if you don't fit, tough.

The status quo is never going to fit us. The only way forward is to stop trying to squeeze ourselves into a size that is simply wrong, and instead, create something new.

What about the men in our lives? Are they consciously forcing this energetic torture upon us? More often than not, I suspect, they are oblivious. The world fits them and they never stop to think how it might feel different to a woman; they are rarely empathic or aware enough to move beyond their own experience of life. It never occurs to them that all the male definitions and standards undermine women at the deepest level; any woman who expresses how she feels is accused of being over-sensitive or hormonal, or is dismissed in any number of other ways. This is perhaps the biggest block to shifting the 'perfection is male' status quo. While the status quo gives men both power and a comfortable world made for them, it will only be the most enlightened of them who open their eyes and push for change.

Our perfection

Perfection isn't male. Perfection comes when we embrace precisely who we are: every aspect, every power, every nuance and every imperfection. Our perfection is female. Whether your version of 'female' is sensitive and feminine, or strong and charismatic, or a sensual Earth Mother, you have the right to live as exactly that, being exactly you. It's our right to love the feminine, to celebrate all our female powers, and never to feel we must reject any aspect of ourselves to conform to a masculine world that is not aligned with who we are.

The world simply hasn't yet allowed a female definition of perfection, and women have suffered hugely as a result. We now have the tools to change this, not by being loud and angry, but by reactivating our powers and creating a new paradigm for ourselves. Read on and I'll show you how you can do this in your own life and the world.

6
The Web Of Limitation

Grace and George stood in front of the first challenge. To reach the next level, they needed to solve the puzzle, find the combination, build the contraption and ring the bell within the allotted time. George stood poised and ready to go. Grace sighed in frustration. How on earth was she going to complete the task with this straitjacket on? How could she build anything with her hands restrained? How could she solve the puzzle while blindfolded, and how would she get to the bell with her feet shackled? How was this fair or right in any way, shape or form?

'Why am I tied up?' she complained.

'Because, although we know that George is your superior in every way, we have to eliminate the slight possibility that you might win,' said the adjudicator. 'On your marks, set, go!'

George leapt into action. Grace tried to move and fell over.

The web of relative limits and sex

By this point, I imagine your mind is positively boggling at the enormity of what we women have to fight against every single day. You're not wrong; it is huge, and grossly unfair.

I'm afraid we aren't at the bottom of the rabbit hole yet. There's another factor, the pièce de résistance, you might say. This one I call the 3D Spider's Web of Limitation – imagine the proverbial 'glass ceiling' but taken to the nth degree.

Patriarchy has always required that women be less than men and has insisted that our purpose is to support and serve. We must have less success, earn less money, have less power, less influence, less freedom, less choice; the final authority must rest with the man. This has created a relative dynamic between men and women in society, and these programmes are underpinned by subconscious beliefs about sex. Whenever women pull themselves out of these limits and begin to equal or outshine the men, they trigger the male subconscious to go into meltdown because their virility is threatened. We also hold the female version of this in our minds; if we become too powerful, the human race will die out because all the men will become impotent. Ridiculous.

These programmes are obviously not conscious, because the light of reason immediately tells us that this is utter rubbish. They lurk deep in the subconscious where they can act unseen; they are insidious, hidden and extremely powerful. This creates a subconscious compulsion for a man to put down a powerful woman, to avoid feeling emasculated. It creates a subconscious compulsion in a woman to limit herself for fear of triggering retribution.

Let's be clear, here. Not all men will act on these archaic programmes. Far from it. Many enlightened men are actively fighting against them, just as women are. Unfortunately, though, there is enough of this energy still active in our group consciousness that women are undermined by it again and again. Remember, our subconscious choices are made based on what we feel, and if we perceive danger, that is enough to hold us back.

The pattern of powerful women threatening these limits in society, and being destroyed as a result, is well documented throughout history. Where women have challenged these limits, they have invariably brought the full force of the status quo down upon themselves, and often in the most violent of ways. For centuries, it's happened over and over again, the persecution of witches being the most extreme example. Sadly, in many cultures, violence is still condoned and sanctioned against women who violate patriarchal limits, both written and unwritten.

It is this Web of Limitation, this web of energetic
boundaries, that forbids women from equalling or
surpassing men, that keeps us blocked and holds us back.
This problem is bigger than you can possibly imagine. This
is the energetic straitjacket we must escape from.

The thermostat of control

Think of the thermostat on your central heating, with
the maximum temperature set. The heating turns on
and starts to heat your house. As soon as the limit is
reached, an automatic mechanism is triggered and the
boiler turns off, stopping the temperature from going
over the limit.

Women's relative limits work in the same way. We decide to go after the goal of growing our business. We strategise, promote our work, get more clients, and everything appears to be going well. Then we reach an invisible limit, and suddenly self-sabotage kicks in at an energetic level. Fears arise. Obstacles sabotage our efforts. The website goes down. We get ill. Impostor syndrome creeps in and asks 'Who do you think you are to believe you can do this?' Before we know where we are, everything has ground to a standstill.

If we look beneath the surface, it's most likely that a relative limit, such as, 'I can only be 60% as success-ful as my husband, or I'll be punished,' has kicked in. Or maybe, 'I'm forbidden from outshining my male colleague.' I've seen brilliant women held back and sabotaged by ridiculous relative limits such as these, time and time again.

As a woman, you will have thousands of relative lim-its programmed deep in your subconscious mind. Limits you would never consciously obey, but which are the hidden thermostat on your success. These are the programmes that carry those extreme and often violent subconscious labels I mentioned earlier, such as a penalty of death. Exceeding these limits is labelled as forbidden and dangerous, and triggers deep ances-tral fears in your subconscious. They can still stop us in our tracks today.

This phenomenon is explained brilliantly by Gay Hendricks in his book *The Big Leap*, which I highly recommend. The point I'm flagging up here is that women have a whole additional matrix of limitations to overcome because of what patriarchy has created. These rigid invisible barriers try to stop us from equalling and outshining men in practically all aspects of life. More often than not, these limits are set relative to the men in our lives – our husbands, partners, brothers and fathers. My husband is nothing but supportive of my career, and has certainly never suggested I should stay in his shadow, and yet I've still had to clear limit after limit on this subject from my subconscious mind. We are fighting against a legacy of staying in the shadows relative to men, and those energies are far from gone.

I expect you think you aren't affected by relative limits, so here are some numbers to convince you. Out of all the clients I've worked one-to-one with in the last three years, 100% had the subconscious belief 'I'm forbidden from outshining men,' and 87% subconsciously believed 'If I outshine men I'll be put to death.'

Think about what that's actually like. Everything we want to do likely triggers a whole host of limits, each one subconsciously associated with punishment and extreme danger. It's like being stuck in a three-dimensional spider's web. You know the direction you want to move your arm in, but as soon as you try, the web pulls you back. You try to move your leg, again the web pulls you back. The web is holding us in a mesh of limits defined by the obsolete past. Any movement to try and free ourselves creates a subconscious backlash. This is the reality of being a twenty-first century woman fighting against the energetic legacy of our history. This is why we get stuck.

CLIENT STORY: JESS

Let me introduce you to Jess. She was a single mother of two grown daughters when I met her. She had started a company after her divorce and, working twenty-four-seven, had built it into a thriving business. On the face of it, she was not a woman held back by old patriarchal conditioning and limitations. She had embraced her role confidently and hadn't taken any rubbish from men as she'd grown her business. Things then started to go wrong. She began to feel stress and anxiety, things which had never troubled her before. At the same time, her company started to have problems: a court case, a tax issue, difficulties with clients. It seemed that everything she had built was falling apart.

She was astonished, and disbelieving, when I told her that she had hit patriarchal limitations and these were causing her to sabotage her success – a reaction I often get. However, under the surface, we found exactly what I had expected. Everything she was doing was labelled as forbidden. Having a business, being outside the home, being in a position of authority, earning a lot of money – or indeed, any money at all. These things were all subconsciously forbidden to her. She had pushed forward, despite these labels, until her success had crossed an invisible limit. We looked into this, and it turned out her subconscious had forbidden her from being more successful than her ex (a successful businessman). What is more, as soon as she reached the limit, her subconscious started telling her that she'd be attacked and killed for daring to surpass this limit.

As with all deep conditioning and programming, Jess knew nothing about it on a conscious level. All she felt was the anxiety, stress and blockages.

This is how we are so easily controlled by old program-ming. If we had the chance to shine the harsh light of reality on these things, before the programmes trigger the fear response, we would immediately see them as illusions, hangovers from obsolete times. But because the fear triggers first, and because most people have no means of identifying what is going on under the surface, these ancient programmes continue to control us.

After removing those limits, updating her subconscious understanding and pulling her power back from her ex, Jess's anxiety and stress disappeared, and so did the sabotaging energies undermining her success.

Stress, strain and fracture

Now that you understand how relative limits work, you can begin to grasp the enormous internal conflict this creates within every woman. As we try to achieve in life, we inevitably hit these invisible limits again and again. Each time you have hit an obstacle, a brick wall, or sabotage in your business or career, this is what has happened. So, what do we do? We push harder and harder, of course. The more we push, the more our subconscious mind tries to pull us back. It's a self-sabotaging nightmare that becomes self-destruction.

I experienced this in academia. I pushed myself more and more to succeed, and I surpassed countless relative limits. Each one set up a cascade of sabotage, trying to force me back into a subservient position. The hidden programming from all those 'forbidden' labels put my body into a perpetual state of fear. Ultimately, my system simply couldn't sustain this and my health broke down. Even though this happened to me decades ago, and you'd assume things are better for women now, it is not the case. Week after week, women with the same problems contact me in need of help. The problem is still very real.

It is because we fight, and refuse to obey those hidden rules, that we create enormous stress within ourselves. Stress creates strain; strain means that things are stretched. We are being pulled in opposite directions. Simple physics tells us that only a certain amount of strain can be tolerated before something breaks. It could be your health (physical or mental), your relationships, your business, your career.

The only way to have the success and freedom we deserve, while keeping our wellbeing intact, is to learn how to extricate ourselves from the Web of Limitation.

EXERCISE: IDENTIFY YOUR WEB OF LIMITATION

As modern women, we don't like to think of ourselves as being held back by patriarchal limits. Usually, we fight this idea to our last breath. Right? However, I bet that deep in the energy matrix of your life you are still obeying these limits.

Use this exercise to identify where the 3D Spider's Web of Limitation is acting as your straitjacket.

1. Who are the key adult men in your life from childhood (father, grandfathers, uncles, older brothers)?

2. Make a note of how you would quantify their success, income, wealth, status, visibility in the world, freedom, opportunity and leadership.

3. Now consider where the key adult women in your childhood (mother, grandmothers, aunts, older sisters) were in comparison with the men. This will show you the familial patterns running during your most impressionable years.

4. Now I want you to look at the same pattern in your current adult life. How does your success, status, income, leadership, freedom and opportunity compare with all the key men in your life? (Include brothers, partners and ex-partners.)

What you will find is one of two possibilities: either you have indeed been held back by invisible limits, such that you cannot outshine the key men in your life, or, you have pushed past these limits.

If it is the latter, I need to ask you an important question. In the relationships where you have equalled, surpassed or outshone a man, is there also conflict, contention, estrangement or resentment between you and the man in question? If so, this is a clear indicator that you have triggered negative programming by surpassing those traditional relative limits.

The essential takeaway is: wherever you have been held back, it was because you were fighting, subconsciously, to free yourself. It was never because you were useless, not good enough or lazy. The more you fight, the more you experience this problem. The more limited you have felt, the more amazing you truly are.

7
The Water Torture

Grace had started off that morning in high spirits, so excited that this was the start of her journey to success. She had spent more time than usual choosing her outfit and doing her hair. She wanted to make a good impression, to look professional and credible. George, she had noted, was also bright, cheerful and smartly attired.

But now, after six hours of clambering through the undergrowth, scrambling through ditches and clinging to rope bridges, she looked like something the cat might have dragged in – hair like a bird's nest, complete with leaves, snags and rips in her frock, and dirt all over her face. She was exhausted and distinctly annoyed. So much for an elegant entrance!

George had hardly broken a sweat strolling along his flowery path.

Little things add up

The most insignificant incident becomes intolerable if repeated a thousand times.

How do our mind and body learn how we should react in a particular situation? My entire journey, from walking through the gates of my college at Cambridge, to this moment, has taught me one essential fact. We are conditioned by the energetic messages we take on from the people and places around us. These signals imprint themselves in our very being and determine the automatic reactions which define our lives. Let's look at this in a little more detail.

How many times have you been stung by a sexist comment or attitude? How many times have you felt anger at a woman's treatment? If you begin to analyse it, you'll find these incidents are as plentiful as grains of sand on the beaches of the world. Equally, have you noticed how often we are told by the world that we are over-reacting, being over-sensitive, that we're an angry feminist or 'man-hater', when we call people out on sexist behaviour? The attitudes behind these responses take incidents at face value and in isolation, and do not look beneath the surface, understand the big picture, or look at the cumulative effect. This dismissive attitude has a profoundly poisonous effect on our wellbeing. We are suffering endless attacks, but aren't allowed to acknowledge them.

The same message given over and over in a million different ways, over decades, will inevitably imprint itself on you and define your reaction to the world. Here are a few of my experiences which perfectly illustrate this point.

1979: I've been put up a year at school and, at the tender age of ten, I'm in a physics lesson at the local comprehensive school. The male teacher says to me, 'You can't expect to beat the boys at physics, Anne.' I'm puzzled. The concept of sexism is new to me. I go home that night and ask why I can't beat the boys. My mother is furious, and rightly so. (At the end of that year, I came top of the class and beat every one of the boys.)

1987: It is my undergraduate matriculation dinner at Cambridge. Above the high table at my college is the Latin inscription: 'How good and delightful it is to live together as brothers in unity.' The Master (head of college) makes a joke about it. At the time, I laugh with everyone else, but looking back what subconscious message did this send me?

1988: I am sitting in a first-year undergraduate lecture on crystallography along with 300 other students. There I was, surrounded by my male friends, listening to the male lecturer. (Perhaps he still remembers my end of course feedback form!) He's talking about electrostatic charges on ions. 'And these are negatively charged, so they must be female!' he chuckles. All my male friends think it's hilarious. I don't. They think my reaction is even funnier and go off to lunch laughing at me. I feel hurt and angry. 'It's just a joke,' they think. 'Why is Anne making a fuss about it?' Yet, here we are, thirty-two years later, and that joke still stings.

1990: I graduated with a first-class honours degree, and came top in the written papers. My department decided to put me forward for the Royal Charter Prize, of the Institute of Metals. I went down to London for the interview, against the other top graduates in the country – all men – and I won the prize. The awards ceremony was in Wales, in a castle. Off I went, with my boyfriend, to receive my award. There were about 200 people in the room. There were just three women: an admin woman from the institute, the girlfriend of the man who had won 'Technician of the Year', and me. Every single person I met assumed that my boyfriend had won the prize. It was clear that no man in that room could comprehend that I, a young woman with long hair, dangly earrings and a flowery dress, could be the winner. Not only that, the comments and whistles from the floor after the alcohol began to flow, were entirely base and utterly inappropriate. Where was the respect that a male winner would have automatically commanded in that situation? It certainly wasn't offered to me.

1991: I'm now doing my PhD, and my supervisor has organised a conference. I and a few of his other research students are helping out, loading the slides and handing out microphones. It comes to coffee time and everyone engages my fellow student, Andy, in conversation, asking him about how his research project is going. Everyone ignores me and assumes I'm an 'admin girl'. I'm deeply offended. Andy and I are performing the same tasks, yet he's clearly a scientist because he's male. I'm invisible.

1991: I am in the department workshop speaking to one of the technicians about getting my composite specimens machined. I'm trying to concentrate while, mere inches from my head, is a nude 'page three' pin-up. Am I supposed to be OK with this? Is it acceptable to have pictures of women as merely sexual objects undermining my status as a serious scientist, literally in my face, like this?[5] How can this man look at that picture and see me next to it, without imagining what I look like naked? I feel deeply uncomfortable. (I doubt there's a woman on the planet who hasn't experienced something like this.)

1992: In the lab again, a film is being made to illustrate a scientific model. I overhear the academic in charge of the project speaking. 'And of course, we need to get a man to do the voice-over. We want it to be taken seriously.' Does a woman's voice automatically have no credibility? Smoke comes out of my ears from repressed fury.

---

5   I should add here that, following complaints from female postgraduates, the department forbade naked pin-ups from being displayed.

1996: I'm now a lecturer in mechanics of materials. The phone rings.

ME: Hello.

MAN: Can I speak to Dr Whitehouse, please?

ME: Yes, speaking.

MAN: [Pause] Oh...

Clearly, in his head, Dr Whitehouse is a man and I am the secretary. (If I had £1 for every time this has happened to me, I'd have retired to the Bahamas by now.)

2001: I have just resigned from my lectureship due to chronic fatigue syndrome. One of my colleges tells me 'You can't leave, Anne, how am I going to get through staff meetings without being able to look at your legs?' Six years of hard work and high-quality scientific contribution and this is how I'm seen.

2019: Things have come full circle and I'm attending an alumni dinner back at my Cambridge college. 2019 is the fortieth anniversary of women being admitted to the college, and the first female Master in the college's 500-year history has just been elected. You would think that these important events might have changed people's expectations about women being entitled to be there. However, as my husband and I introduce ourselves to an older man, he immediately turns to my husband, ignoring me completely, and says, 'I assume you are the graduate.'

We put him straight quickly enough, but the fact remains that when he looked at us, he automatically assigned the status to my husband. Clearly, I *still* do not look like a scholar, graduate, prize-winner, post-graduate, and postdoctoral research fellow – my actual credentials during my time at the college – simply because I am female. But of course, perfection is male and I am the wrong shape.

Betraying the sisterhood

Not only do we have men to contend with, but other women can also undermine us, accusing us of betrayal and exacerbating the problem. One glance at social media and you'll find an army of so-called 'badass' women, with posts filled with swearing and aggressive affirmations. While I understand all too well that this has been their survival mechanism, this isn't true power. In my system, such women are warrior archetypes, whose underlying foundation is just as disempowered as any of us. Their coping mechanism is to take on the antagonistic energy of the wounded male. This doesn't make them empowered women, although they clearly believe they are.

I've had such women lash out at me many times because I dare to suggest that women are still disempowered by the past, that we have deep-seated conditioning that makes us submit on the energetic level, and that we fall victim to these hidden energies. This is despite my decades of meticulous work and analysis that led me to these conclusions. In the past, I have been afraid of speaking up because of this. Not very empowered of me, I know. Understandable, though – it's hard to be attacked from all sides.

These women misunderstand the truth, of course. They think that by acknowledging how undermined we are, and how negatively it can affect us, we are admitting we're weak. Far from it. It is only when we start to prove how gifted and how strong we are, and so trigger all those limits and labels, that all this sabotage kicks in. We should be getting medals. The more you're affected, the more amazing a woman you are, because it demonstrates, beyond any doubt, your resilience, strength, aspiration, determination and talent.

Cumulative damage

Little incidents, but many of them, over and over again, cause cumulative damage. Each one undermining, mocking, telling us, 'You shouldn't be here. This is for men only. You will never be good enough, credible, respected. We've let you in, but don't think we accept you as an equal.' It's the patriarchal version of dripping water torture. You can brush these experiences off to start with but, accumulated over years, they become deeply insulting and undermining; they eat away at you.

Little incidents matter. They matter because they antagonise The Beast we're fighting against every single moment. They trigger all those programmes of 'this is forbidden' and 'perfection is male', which we are striving to suppress. Each time something like this happens, our minds and bodies perceive it, energetically, as a censure for being who we are. It undermines us at a far deeper level than the world acknowledges.

By the time we reach adulthood, pre-programmed evolutionary responses and feminine wounds have taken away our true power and locked us into an automatic submissive response. What follows is decades of this energetic onslaught, each incident magnifying and adding to the last. Whenever we move forward in the world, when we step up, shine and outshine, we receive an energetic backlash with the overwhelming message: 'This is forbidden for you.'

My experiences are typical of any woman trying to succeed in a 'man's world'. Even if your environment is no longer male-dominated, more than likely it used to be, and the energetic legacy is still screaming 'perfection is male' at you, undermining you in a million different ways.

Drip, drip, drip…

When the underlying message we receive day in day out is that we aren't allowed to be there, that we aren't as good as the men, and that we can't possibly command the same credibility, respect and status, it's no wonder women don't feel the confidence that our abilities and qualifications should give us. On the surface, this can and does act as a motivation for us to get out there and prove them wrong. It certainly did for me, for many years, but I didn't realise what was happening. I didn't realise that my motivation came at the cost of being undermined at a profound level.

Now it's your turn. Think now about the repeated negative messages you have received in your life up to now. How has this affected the way you see yourself and the world? How has this affected your confidence, the way you present and promote yourself? How has it limited or sabotaged your choices?

We aren't doing this to point fingers or attack individuals. The historic legacy which created our struggle is nothing to do with individuals and certainly does not incriminate the entire male gender.[6] Never confuse the underlying legacy conditioning – which we all share – with individual people. Attacking people achieves little of lasting value. It just triggers more resistance and perpetuates resentment. We need to be more enlightened. Instead, it's about understanding

---

6 Individual men can either go along with the status quo programming, without discernment, or they can step up and challenge the injustice wherever they find it, fighting their own subconscious conditioning in the process. Many men are doing exactly this.

the factors that have held you back and taken away your power. Once you see the truth, you can begin to transform those patterns and free yourself using the tools I'll be showing you later. This is the way to change the energetic power dynamic of our society and to level the playing field for all women.

Next time someone tells you you're over-reacting, give them this book.

8

Female Power Archetypes

Grace stood, rooted to the spot, with The Beast growling and looming over her. Saliva dripped from its fangs. She could even hear its stomach rumbling as it looked at her hungrily. Her heart pounded in her chest.

What was she to do now? She couldn't confront The Beast on its own terms. She simply wasn't the size of a small barn with vicious claws and a temperament to match. Yet she had to survive somehow.

Grace considered her options: a large beast tranquiliser gun would have been nice, but there didn't seem to be one handy. What else could she do? She could attempt to fight. She could run. She could hide. She could keep very still and hope The Beast would get bored and wander off. None of these options seemed satisfactory, but she needed to pick one if she wanted to live.

Compensating to survive

You now understand The Beast you have been fighting against all these years. It's powerful, it's insidious and it can destroy you if you don't know how to deal with it. Every woman comes up against and is undermined by The Beast, and we tend to compensate in one of five distinct ways. These are my Female Power Archetypes.

Each archetype represents a journey from disempowered to empowered. You may find that you move from one archetype to another over time. Understanding your archetype helps you understand your power story. It helps you to acknowledge how courageous you are, and it also points the way to where your potential can take you. These archetypes have no relationship whatsoever to any other archetype systems you may be familiar with. They are based entirely on the patterns I've identified within my clients and, indeed, in myself.

The five main archetypes are Rapunzel, Cinderella, Snow White, Hippolyta and Scheherazade. Each represents a particular compensation mechanism that enables us to survive and achieve. However, each comes with a cost because when we are compensating, we aren't perfectly aligned with who we are. There's also a sixth archetype, whom we'll meet later on.

Before we go any further, I can already sense your protests at my choosing, for the most part, fairy tale heroines – characters who, on the face of it, do not represent modern women in any way, shape or form, and in whom that old paradigm of the weak female, in need of rescue, is entrenched.

Fear not. This is not what I am promoting here. On the contrary, this is done quite deliberately and all will become clear.

Let's meet the archetypes.

Rapunzel

In the fairy tale, Rapunzel is kept imprisoned, away from life, love and the world. She is limited and controlled. She longs to escape and embrace her life. She yearns for freedom.

If you are the Rapunzel Power Archetype, your biggest challenge is overcoming the limitations that have been imposed on you. These might be physical limitations, but more likely they are the energetic limitations of patriarchal attitudes, cultures and beliefs. These keep you small, restricted and they stop your power and light from shining over your life and in the world.

As a Rapunzel Power Archetype, you've been brought up in an environment where old gender inequalities still prevail. Men have the power. Men control the women, either directly or indirectly. This might mean you come from a patriarchal culture or a family in which women are treated as second-class citizens. It might mean you're limited to particular roles in life and don't have the freedom to choose what you do. It might mean that you have choice and freedom to some extent, but men still enforce their dominance. It might mean that your parents 'wanted a son' and you've always been made to feel not good enough. Or perhaps you weren't given the same opportunities and freedoms as your brother.

This pattern of disempowerment exists in many guises, but the result is always the same. You're in a prison, which tells you women should be controlled, hidden and that your freedom is forbidden. You probably struggle to speak up; each time you try to move forward, blocks and fears stop you in your tracks because you're energetically restrained. But this prison isn't real; it's a prison of old beliefs and attitudes, which need to go – and the sooner the better.

People tend to think that the Rapunzel type is weak, but this isn't the case at all. Rapunzels can become the greatest pioneers and the most inspirational leaders. These are the women this planet needs. It doesn't matter where you live or what your society is like, Rapunzel's empowerment shines through.

An example of an empowered Rapunzel is Malala Yousafzai, the girl who was shot by the Taliban for demanding an education. She's now a world-changing inspiration and the youngest recipient of the Nobel Peace Prize to date. A Rapunzel can create shifts in attitudes and understanding which spread like wildfire.

Here's your big motivation, and the light to hold on to when things are difficult: you are the catalyst that can help bring freedom and fulfilment to millions of women. You're the kind of woman who, when you finally embrace your power, becomes the most amazing, pioneering leader. You can change the world.

Cinderella

The downtrodden, disempowered, invisible heroine who learns to shine and step into her true power. For a Cinderella, it doesn't matter where you've come from or what you've been through. The more you've been held back, the brighter you can shine.

Cinderella's journey is one of pain transformed into brilliance, of disempowerment turned into inspiration. Of all the Female Power Archetypes, Cinderella has the most potential for transformation. Any Cinderella-type will have been through some challenging or painful experiences. This might have been a difficult childhood, of abandonment, being put

111

down or crushed in one way or another, or it might have been major trauma and abuse, loss or bereavement – the big stuff.

As a Cinderella Power Archetype, you've been crushed by life to a greater or lesser extent. This means you've been wounded mentally, physically or emotionally by aggressive, oppressive, domineering or violent energy in one form or another. You have severe feminine wounds. When this happens to us, we go into survival mode – we shut down our inner spark and shift toward invisibility and powerlessness.

At the beginning of your Cinderella power journey, instead of shining your light into the world and receiving all the love, attention and recognition you deserve, you're behind the scenes, pleasing others, keeping your head down, and allowing others to have all the power in your life. You dread confrontation and criticism, and you stop yourself from outshining others, even though you would love to. This leads to stress, anxiety, unhappiness and frustration. The Cinderella route to empowerment is a journey from victim to inspiration. When our minds are stuck in victim mode – blaming others, or 'life did this to me' – we lock ourselves into powerlessness. Nothing can change.

You can choose to adopt a higher perspective. The more you've been pushed down, the greater your potential to transform. Anyone who has had their feminine power crushed will naturally develop the gifts of compassion, kindness, sensitivity, empathy, inner strength, resilience and so much more. Beyond that, it also develops your psychic gifts. It's the process of alchemy that I love so much, and which I've nurtured many women through over the years.

Your experiences are your training course to become the most amazing version of yourself possible. The reason you've experienced difficult things isn't that you deserved it. It's because you were strong enough to do more than merely survive. You were strong enough to live through hard experiences and transform them into something incredible. Your task is to find and nurture that brilliance within yourself.

When your Cinderella power is flowing, you are the most inspirational of women. You've found an inner strength and determination many thought impossible. You've rejected your negative programming about the world, about your value, and about your right to be seen and heard. You've embraced the truth that you are amazing, worthwhile, and have wonderful gifts to share.

Your big motivation, and the light to hold on to when things are difficult for you, is to imagine the woman who hasn't yet found this strength, who hasn't managed to turn things around for herself and is stuck in powerless invisibility, thinking there's no hope for her. Imagine you meet her by chance and end up sharing a coffee. Just seeing what you've become, after what you've been through, can open up a whole new world for her. When we see something is possible, our mind immediately begins to recreate our reality and allow in a million new possibilities. Maybe there's a woman out there who is just waiting to meet you.

Snow White

The Snow White archetype is related to Cinderella. Snow White was attacked by the wicked stepmother because of her beauty, and this is the key point. She is the woman who has suffered, been discriminated against, been used or disregarded because of her body, her beauty or her sexual attractiveness. She may have experienced rape, abuse or trauma, and, if so, her experiences will have led to deep-rooted and possibly self-destructive negative conditioning. Alternatively, it may simply be that she has been brought up in an environment where women are only valued for their bodies and their attractiveness to men; their intellect, heart, and soul are not recognised.

When a woman has been disempowered in this way, she will have shut down her true female power, as we all do to some extent, but, in her case, everything becomes focused on her body. This woman is susceptible to eating disorders and body image problems. She may have self-harmed. Her understanding of love will be distorted at the deepest level, and her self-worth inextricably tied up in her physical appearance. She may feel she has to offer sex to be loved or accepted. Or, she may have blocked out any human intimacy to keep herself safe.

Snow White's journey is one to understand her inner beauty and intrinsic value; the understanding that what she has gone through, and how other people have objectified her, in no way changes her value as a human being. This usually requires deep healing and transformation. The reactivation of inner power, if you are a Snow White archetype, is particularly profound, and completely shifts your understanding of life.

Hippolyta, queen of the Amazon warriors

Hippolyta is the warrior queen of the Amazons in Greek mythology, daughter of Ares, God of War, who led her warrior women into battle and was a force to be reckoned with.

If you're a Hippolyta archetype you are a woman who has chosen the warrior path. This might have been a natural choice based on your character, or it may have been the only option for your survival. You may have started out as a Rapunzel or a Cinderella but then rebelled against your experiences; instead of making yourself invisible, you replaced your female energy with male energy. Often, a Hippolyta will have confused wounded female power with true flowing female power and labelled it as weak. Or maybe you simply emulate male energy, because it has provided a way to succeed. Either way, you have taken on a more male power to get what you want from life.

Patriarchy is nothing to you. No matter your upbringing or culture, you have blasted through any beliefs or rules that say you're less than men. You aren't held back by rules that don't suit you. Energetic barriers that would sabotage and undermine most women are nothing to you. You probably don't even notice them. But they are still there, and even Hippolyta will sometimes find herself held back by blocks and glass ceilings.

Your confidence and self-assurance are the envy of many. You thrive in a competitive environment and adore exciting new experiences. You're a natural leader and command a room easily and effortlessly, whether giving a speech or chairing a board meeting. You slip easily and effortlessly into roles with authority and men likely feel intimidated by you much of the time.

However, there is often a cost. If your power is too male dominant, you can become overly aggressive, intolerant and insensitive. Hippolyta types often fail to understand that not all women are warriors, and what you have blasted through does indeed undermine and crush other women – not because they are intrinsically weak, but because their life experiences and character created a different reaction to The Beast at a young age. It is important that you acknowledge this and don't dismiss other women's genuine reactions to life, just because they are different from yours.

You have probably been using 'fight' energy to provide your motivation and strength. While this certainly gets results, it's not a good idea to live your whole life in this way; this energy blocks love, wellbeing and abundance in the long-term. It's more than that, though. The truth is, your female power is a part of you, and when you reactivate it and temper the male energy with your female gifts, you will become even more impressive. Blocking or ignoring any aspect of yourself will only undermine you and limit your achievements. Suppressing your natural power is also very exhausting and invariably creates a feeling of incessant struggle in your life. Feeling that life is a struggle and a battle is a sign that you haven't activated your full power. Fully embracing your feminine side can only enhance who you are and enable you to more fully realise your potential in life.

In many ways you are lucky because your natural reaction has saved you from most of the difficult challenges the other archetypes have to face. However, you can make things even better for yourself by fully activating every aspect of your power.

When a Hippolyta type has truly balanced her power, she is the woman who no longer needs to fight, because not only does she command respect, she breaks down the old structures and builds the new like a force of nature.

Scheherazade

Scheherazade is the heroine of *The Arabian Nights*, who told the 1001 tales under the threat of death and used her intellect to save herself. If you're this archetype, you are a woman who is driven to succeed and push past boundaries, but at a heavy personal cost. If you're a Scheherazade, you are a woman who is out in the world, yearning to achieve and shine. You're also sensitive, feminine, a deep thinker. You're probably naturally quiet.

This is the problem. Scheherazade is energetically highly aware of all the subtle energies labelling things as forbidden. She's subconsciously aware of the Spider Web of Limitation. She's shut down her female power and has squashed herself into the patriarchy box. She had to do to this to survive and get this far. But, because she is so sensitive, this triggers messages of danger in her mind and body. In turn, this triggers a fight or flight response. Her body tells her over and over again that she's going to be punished for daring to violate the patriarchal laws of the energy matrix. She is locked into a submission response, depriving her of confidence and making her feel permanently under attack.

She is the woman who struggles with confidence, who holds back or has to screw up her courage and force herself to endure ordeals. She is the woman who agonises over every bit of criticism and becomes locked into a pattern of self-destructive perfectionism. She isn't a warrior. She isn't angry and rebellious. Yet she's put herself in the lion's den of aggressive energies because of her drive to succeed and prove herself. She's between a rock and a hard place. She may well appear incredibly successful on the surface, but inside she's being eaten away by The Beast.

I am a Scheherazade archetype myself. The majority of my clients are Scheherazades. We are the achievers, but we are also in great danger of burning out, suffering from chronic fatigue, anxiety and stress. If we don't sort our power out, we are a disaster waiting to happen.

In my journey through academia, I met mostly warriors and a few Scheherazades like me. Without exception, the warriors had unbalanced power and had given up their femininity to take on the establishment with a degree of success, and the Scheherazades were achieving on the surface, but suffering with stress, anxiety and low self-confidence underneath – without exception. Even yesterday, as I was writing this, another typical Scheherazade entered my private practice – a professional woman, suffering with anxiety, panic attacks and depression. When we got into her subconscious mind, I found exactly what

I expected: she subconsciously felt she was doing something forbidden and would be executed. This needs to change, and now. Thankfully, in her case, we are already changing it.

Why fairy tales?

It is appropriate that I've chosen fairy tale characters for the archetypes. We women share the same starting point of a patriarchal legacy, where women are disempowered and limited. In that fairy-tale world, the story usually ends when the heroine is rescued by a man (cringe). We need to acknowledge this before we can take the appropriate action to free ourselves from that legacy. If we deny this fact, we will never address the root effectively. Patriarchy is the truth of our legacy. Acknowledging this in no way suggests we are weak, subservient or inferior. What it does is flag up and acknowledge the hidden battle we must fight to achieve anything.

Don't worry, though – there will be no rescuing in this book.

Understanding your power archetype shows you the compensation mechanism your life experience and character has forced you to adopt. Only by recognising exactly how you have compensated can you discover your most effective route to freedom. The more information you have, the more dramatic the transformation you can make in your life.

Of course, being twenty-first century women, we do not need or intend to be rescued by a man – or by anyone, for that matter. We want true power and true freedom for ourselves. We may start out with the archetypal fairy tale heroine, but we won't take her story to its traditional conclusion. Now that we understand the nature of The Beast, we don't need to be rescued, we can tame The Beast ourselves and claim back our power. We will end the story differently. In the next section, I'll show you how.

9

Female History Syndrome

Grace lay on the ground, looking up at sky, trying to catch her breath. The sinking feeling in her stomach grew stronger. The truth had been staring her in the face the whole time, of course, but she hadn't wanted to believe it. Now, however, there could be no debate.

She was expected to endure, prove and be much more than George, if she wanted to reach the Palace of Success. With so much more on her plate, how would anyone see her true abilities? How would she even appear as good as George? It simply wasn't fair.

Smoke began to come out of her ears as her annoyance transformed into rage – well, metaphorical smoke anyway.

Time for a new definition

Now that we have the whole picture, in all its gory detail, we can finally understand where our struggles and our particular version of impostor syndrome[7] come from. In our conscious minds, we are determined to embrace our rights, fulfil our potential and use our gifts. We push forward and create the careers, businesses and achievements we know we are capable of. We are fully aware of the freedoms and rights we have today, and how lucky we are – on the surface, at least – compared with our female forebears. This all creates drive, motivation and a hunger to prove ourselves that pushes us forward and stops us from giving up.

Yet it's a double-edged sword. You now understand that, under the surface, our natural responses, our conditioning and the energetic messages we're bombarded with left, right and centre, keep screaming at us, 'Forbidden. Danger. Punishment. Limits. No. No. No.' There's no power foundation under our feet. Our bodies perceive extreme danger and go into survival mode, locking us into a submissive, fight or flight high-alert state, which undermines our physical and mental wellbeing.

Wherever we turn in the world, the message 'perfection is male' still feeds that never-ending conditioning. 'You are imperfect. You can never be what is required. You will always be less. You must get back to where you belong. Your feminine nature and way of doing things aren't acceptable.'

---

7   I believe that impostor syndrome is invariably caused by a lack of power foundation, and so can have various roots. The particular variant we are concerned with here is the gender version.

So we shut down even more parts of ourselves and squeeze deeper into that patriarchy box, trying to conform and turn ourselves into something we can never be. We feel incomplete. We are energetically constrained from all sides, our confidence is undermined further, and we feel even less safe. But all this is going on under the surface and we don't understand why we feel the way we do.

Then our reasoning kicks in. Why aren't we feeling confident? Why aren't we flourishing as we should be? Why are our male peers relaxed when we feel as if we're going to the guillotine? We must not be trying hard enough. We're in danger of proving women are less than men, that women are weaker and less capable. Destructive perfectionism kicks in and we force ourselves onwards. Meanwhile, every step forward sends our subconscious minds and bodies further into panic.

It's no wonder something inevitably breaks.

This not only explains the deep insecurity that undermines women's confidence and makes us feel we're not good enough, it also explains why we feel like impostors. We *are* impostors, because we are not men, yet we live within an energetic matrix which uses male parameters. But the word 'impostor' doesn't describe the full picture and the real battle we are all fighting. As of now, I am renaming it. Impostor syndrome is no more. We are suffering from Female History Syndrome. Here is the full definition:

Female History Syndrome is the deep energetic undermining of aspirational women who, while pushing forward to embrace their rights and fulfil their potential in life, are subtly undermined by a lack of a historical power foundation, by subconscious conditioning from the patriarchal past forbidding them from claiming their rights and freedoms, and by a hardwired energetic submission response. The resulting internal conflict creates stress, anxiety, a lack of confidence and the feeling of being a fraud (what we formerly called impostor syndrome), and may lead to burnout and health problems.

Female History Syndrome is our 'Factor X'. It affects and undermines many, many women, probably you included. It's a condition the conventional world doesn't acknowledge because we 'shouldn't be able to feel' these energies. Yet, the evidence is overwhelming. Women *are* affected by the energies of the past. We are still affected by hidden patriarchal beliefs and prevailing energetic limitations on women. Whether you react by rebelling and pushing yourself toward warrior energy, or you are crushed while forcing yourself to continue, this is the true root of what is undermining your confidence, wellbeing, and achievement.

The legacy of the past drags women down. The more you try to pull away from the archaic definitions and limitations of what women can do and be, the more you will be pulled back. This puts you under enormous strain, a strain no man will ever feel.

Our dilemma

The challenge we face is that these subconscious beliefs and labels, the lack of power foundation, the historical energies of our institutions, shouldn't exist, according to the conventional world, because they are energetic echoes. To the conventional mind, limited to the solid world that we can see, they don't exist in a way that people can perceive, and so how could they possibly have such a huge effect on so many women?

If people don't acknowledge that the problem exists, how will things change? Do we pretend that these energies, beliefs and labels aren't real, to avoid being ridiculed? Do we let people tell us that we have 'made it all up' and, in doing so, allow The Beast to continue sabotaging us and bringing us down, year after year? Or do we decide that our lives, our happiness and our fulfilment are more important, and use the under-standing and tools I'm providing?

If you're in any doubt, let me affirm something. When all this happened to me, I was a 3D, solid world scientist, body and soul. I knew nothing of subtle energies or the subconscious mind. I believed I was limited to the dimensions of my own physical body. However, I knew how I felt. I knew the way my body reacted to the environment I was working in. I knew the feeling of power draining away from me each time I inter-acted in my workplace, even though I didn't know what it was. I knew all too well how it had destroyed my happiness, my health and my career. I was neither pathetic, nor lazy, nor attention-seeking. I was deter-mined, clever and motivated, yet this invisible 'some-thing' pulled the rug out from under me.

If I had believed what the conventional world told me, I would still be lying on that sofa, unable to stand, with chronic fatigue, severe anxiety and pretty much no life at all. Thankfully, I was not prepared to give up. The only alternative was to dig deeper and open my mind to concepts that hadn't seemed possible before. Every layer I discovered, every tool I learnt, every breakthrough I made, I used it, tested it, and got results. Repeatable results. I became an experimental scientist in subtle energy.

I am not a woman of blind faith. I am a woman who needs evidence – repeatable evidence. I am logical and analytical. I need to know why, and how. Even though I am now operating in a non-conventional arena, those principles are still dear to my heart and I apply them in my work, always.

When you have gone through the female power activation process that I'm about to teach you, you will be able to thrive out in the world, even while the old energies prevail, without losing your femininity, your sensitivity or your health, and without having to change your character or behave like a man. It is possible to stay intrinsically you, to reactivate and wield your true female power, to overcome the submission response and feel safe and confident. To start with, all you need is to accept the possibility of the deeper world I have shown you.

PART TWO
THE SIX KEYS TO FEMALE EMPOWERMENT

Knowledge is only the first step to power. Tools that work give you that power.

Whichever Female Power Archetype you are now, I want you to understand one essential fact. You've done brilliantly to get this far, considering The Beast you've been fighting. However, survival and compensation mechanisms can never allow us to truly thrive. We have shut down our true power and stifled our brilliance to conform. When we block any part of ourselves, we are less than we can be, and the world is poorer as a result. It is time to change this, permanently.

In this part of the book, I'll be showing you how to free yourself from those disempowering patterns, how to connect to and activate all of your powers – this includes both those powers that are permitted in the conventional 'perfection is male' world, and those powers that are forbidden, evil, dangerous, all the things wise women were put to death for in the past. Anything that says you must be a certain way, must reject parts of yourself, change who you are, or give up your freedom to have value, is obsolete. This is non-negotiable.

When you find dusty old cobwebs under the bed, you don't revere them and insist they stay there forever. As soon as you become aware of them, you vacuum them away and make everything fresh and clean. The energetic structures of the world and people's subconscious minds also need a darned good vacuuming.

Get ready to free yourself from those straitjackets and activate your true power.[8] To support you with this transformation I have created online audio meditations and energy clearings. Make sure you use them to get the maximum benefit. You can access them here: www.feminineconfidence.com/PullBackYourPowerBonuses

---

8   These techniques are to be used alongside any conventional treatments you may be receiving. Under no circumstances do they replace medical treatment or medication.

10
The New Frontier In Empowerment

Grace had had enough. She'd followed all the rules, done exactly what was expected of her but, right from the beginning, George had been given the easy path and all the advantages. Not only that, everyone else seemed not to notice how much harder it was for her to achieve anything. It wasn't fair, and there was no way on earth that she could equal his success. It was time for drastic and rebellious action.

Grace wasn't a rebel at heart, and she was certainly no warrior, but there comes a time when every woman is pushed to her limit and has to stand up for what is right. It was time to ignore those ridiculous rules and remember how powerful she really was.

When our power archetypes reach their limit, what next?

Let's start by revisiting Scheherazade's story. Scheherazade was daughter of the Grand Vizier, and wife of the Sultan – whose habit was to marry a girl and then behead her the next morning. There she was, living in a world where each morning the possibility of death awaited her. She was in a world controlled by powerful men, where there was no escape. The only thing she had was her intelligence and her storytelling ability. Each night she told a story during the cool hours before dawn, and her sister was primed always to ask her to begin a new story before the sun came up. That way, the Sultan would be eager to hear the end of the story and delay her execution by one more day. (Of course, he ultimately falls in love with her and, when she finally ends her stories after 1001 nights, all is well – but that part of the tale isn't relevant here.)

This is a perfect analogy for our situation. We put ourselves in careers and acquire statuses that are still labelled energetically as being for men alone and forbidden for us. We hear this message, 'This is forbidden – you will be punished', loud and clear every day, and we fight it. We fight it body and soul. This is what triggers the underlying responses of submission, giving away our power, anxiety and stress. I've felt many times as if I were going to my execution when I was simply living through a normal day.

On the surface, you're thinking, 'How can I get that presentation done on time?' Under the surface, your subconscious is thinking, 'How can I survive another day in this forbidden realm without being executed?' On the surface, you're thinking, 'How can I get my work noticed, so I can get that promotion?' Under the surface, your subconscious is thinking, 'How can I be as invisible as possible, so the authorities don't notice I've broken the patriarchy rules and kill me?' We are being pulled inexorably in opposite directions, all the time.

The archetypes we have met so far – Cinderella, Rapunzel, Snow White, Scheherazade and Hippolyta – are the different ways in which we women compensate, survive and cope with having our female power shut down by wounding and conditioning. By adopting one of the archetypes as our compensation mechanism, we have been able to function and succeed up to a point, even while our true power is shut down. However, none of these archetypes shows us the best way to succeed, or how to access our enlightenment and genius zone. They can only take us so far.

The more we push against the old programming, the more internal conflict and strain we create. There will be a point where this approach no longer works and something breaks. If you're a woman who is pushing forward to succeed in life, but you have started to experience anxiety, insomnia, depression, a lack of confidence, financial blocks, relationships falling apart, feeling like a fraud, chronic fatigue or other physical health problems, you have reached the limit of what you can do in your current energy state. Your power compensation mechanism cannot be stretched any further. This was the point I had reached when I had to give up my scientific career. I'd pushed my Scheherazade mechanisms to the maximum until finally, everything imploded and there was nowhere left to go.

If you have been succeeding in life by drawing on Hippolyta warrior energy, then you probably believed you were doing well. When you reach the limit of this archetype, typically one of two things happens. Either you are suddenly hit by anxiety and stress that you have never experienced before, or money issues suddenly appear and pull you down, often in the shape of you being attacked by the establishment. The relationship between money and power is the subject of another book; for now, all you need to understand is that they are inextricably linked.

In the past, once you had reached the limit of your archetype, this was as far as you could go. Thankfully, now that you understand Female History Syndrome, you have another option. The step women have been waiting for, one that is no longer a compromise.

What we need is a way to change the damaging messages coming towards us, to deflect the negativity, change our automatic responses and make it safe to be out in the world, doing what we want to do without limits. All this without turning ourselves into men, aggressive women or anything else alien to our nature. We need to know how to change the energies around us in a way that not only gives us back our power, but which is aligned with our true female nature. This is what I will show you.

The final Female Power Archetype: the Sorceress

It's time to meet our final Female Power Archetype. Enter, the Sorceress. She doesn't have a name. Well, more accurately, her name is *your* name.

The Sorceress is the woman you will be when you no longer have to compensate for power that has been shut down. She is the woman you will be when the damage has been undone, and your true female power has reawakened. To become her, you must unfreeze your past wounds, retrain yourself to stop submitting, and release the fear response of patriarchal conditioning. You must free yourself from the Web of Limitation, get out of the patriarchy box and reactivate all the parts of yourself you suppressed.

When you've done this, you will react differently to life. You'll have a set of powerful tools which will enable you to shift the dynamics of your daily interactions so you feel safe, in alignment with your true power. When you do this, there will be no need to submit or suppress, and no need to be angry or aggressive. You will simply shine as yourself.

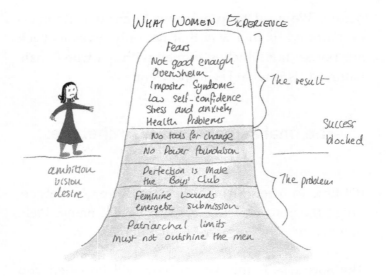

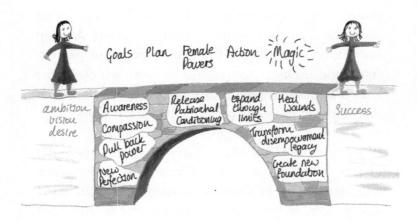

When women set out to succeed, instead of a stone bridge under our feet, we have a mountain to climb. But when we deactivate that disempowering legacy, we can create a firm foundation for success.

When you have become your version of the Sorceress, you will find balance, harmony, power, intuition and inspiration. It is in this energetic state that you will naturally find your zone of greatness, your unique gifts will be in the most fertile ground to flourish, and you will have the confidence to express all this in what you create in the world.

The Sorceress is where we now take our fairy tale. We may start out as the traditional heroine, disempowered and limited, but instead of being rescued, we rediscover our magical powers. When we have these, we can do whatever we want. We can achieve everything of which we are capable. This is our goal.

In the following sections, I'll take you through the process of transforming from your current archetype into the Sorceress. This is my signature process, the 'Six Keys to Female Empowerment'.

Becoming the Sorceress

There will be no magic wand waving here! We are going to meticulously take each aspect of our disempowerment and turn it on its head. In doing this, in the right order and the right way, not only can we free ourselves from the sabotage that's been undermining us, we can create a healthy power foundation for ourselves, which will keep us aligned and safe as we navigate the world.

In the next sections, I'll take you through each key to empowerment in turn and show you how to activate them in your life. Make sure you access the bonus healings and meditations from the online resources page. To get results, you need just three things:

1. The power of your mind.

2. The understanding that everything is energy, everything is connected, and you can instigate change with the power of your mind and body.

3. To take action consistently.

Just one note before we get started: it's essential that you follow the keys in order. You won't receive the same benefits if you pick 'n' mix. We are building a whole new power foundation for your life, and we have to start with the basics first. You cannot build a house by starting with the roof. Please, trust the process, follow it through, and know that *you can* free yourself and shine effortlessly in your life.

Right, let's go.

Harnessing your energetic connection

The first step toward changing your power reaction is to understand and harness your energetic connection with the world around you. Maybe you are already familiar with subtle energies. If you are, brilliant. If this is a new concept for you, don't worry. Just like any muscle, you need to practise using it to become more sensitive and skilled, but you were born with the ability. Everyone can do this.

You can think of your energy field as a finely tuned antenna, picking up all sorts of information from around you. You have been going through your life receiving these signals, processing them subconsciously and allowing them to influence your conscious responses, without knowing it. Think about when you meet someone for the first time and you have an immediate reaction; you take an instant liking to them or perhaps feel deeply uncomfortable. Similarly, I expect there have been times when you've gone into an old building and felt a creepy, uncomfortable vibe. This is your body picking up and processing subtle signals from the energy field around you. You will now be learning to take this to the next level and consciously change the energies around you.

Why is this necessary? Well, I'm sure you understand now that the root of our disempowerment runs deep within the world around us. Simply thinking, visualising or using affirmations won't change anything at this deep power level. Even changing your subconscious beliefs using one of the myriad techniques available, won't go deep enough. I know, because I spent years changing my subconscious programming and, although it helped to a certain extent, the underlying disempowerment and submission response didn't change at all. We need something much deeper, something which not only reaches into the energy of our cells and cleans out all those obsolete labels, but enables us to change the power dynamic between us and the world.

The way to start this process is to use your heart field energy. This is the electromagnetic field around the human heart, which is bigger than the field around your brain. It flows up from your heart, out through the top of your head, around the outside of your body, and then up through your feet in a torus (or dough-nut) shape.

When you connect to your heart field, you bring conscious awareness into your energy field. You can release blocks from your energy field, and enter into active, energetic connection with the world around you. Doing this has many benefits for reducing stress, but when you learn to connect with a conscious inten-tion, you can actively create change too.

In the guided meditations I have provided in this book, you will combine the effects of your heart energy and your mind. This will give you a whole new level of empowerment with which to transform your life.

11
Key One: Awareness

Grace rummaged in her bag and, right at the bottom, her fingers closed around the old spell book her grandmother had passed down to her. As she opened it the ancient pages began to crackle with power. She knew what to do, she knew how to use this power. It was within her. It was part of her. How could she have forgotten?

Grace screwed up the ridiculous rules and cast them aside, pulled off her corset, and steadied herself. The game had changed.

Grace the Sorceress was back!

Know your beast

This is the exciting part. Now you are going to start turning things around for yourself.

The first key to empowerment is *Awareness*. It is awareness that starts to release the power those old programmes had over us, and it is awareness that starts to bring back your power. Awareness brings you the freedom you need to create the change you want. Without awareness, you will be stuck in the same prison for the rest of your life.

When you started reading this book, most likely you had the mindset that you were going to have to put up with things as they were. You doubtless believed that you should be thriving, feeling on top of things, and being a strong modern woman, for whom subservience was a thing of the past. You should be, but you failed, and the reason for your failure must surely be your character. There was something in you that made it impossible to be relaxed, confident and self-assured, and the more you pushed forward into impact, visibility and success, the worse this would get. You probably felt that the fact you suffered these emotional and mental blocks made you intrinsically inferior to those around you who leapt happily up the ladder of success. This would, of course, then lead to endless self-judgement and criticism, which would undermine you further. The downward spiral of doom was well underway.

You should now have a completely different perspective, and understand that:

- When you try to do, be or have anything which takes you away from the role of a traditional woman of your heritage, you find that these things are labelled as forbidden by your subconscious mind. Not only that, as a result of doing them, your subconscious believes that you will be punished, or even executed. This triggers fear and survival responses.

- From childhood, you have been conditioned to give away your power whenever you perceived anything to be a danger. Your default response to life is to go into energetic submission, even if mentally you are pushing forward. This response takes away your power in all of your interactions with the world.

- You are likely to have a whole selection of frozen experiences starting early in childhood where your mind got locked into believing that anything resembling wounded male power (whether in a man, woman or institution) was life-threatening.

- Your subconscious mind does not update on its own. It does not see that you have misinterpreted situations, it does not understand that you're an adult with rights, it does not unfreeze those frozen experiences, and it does not know that you are no longer living in the times of your ancestors. It's pretty hopeless.

The above facts create the subconscious perception that you are in real danger most of the time, triggering your body's survival responses: fight or flight. This is then exacerbated by your lack of power foundation; every cell in your body feels that you lack entitlement to be in any of the roles and places that have traditionally been exclusively for men.

It all becomes more magnified when the 'perfection is male' water torture comes into play. At this point, my experience tells me that most women shut down their unique female powers, and force themselves into the patriarchy box. From this point onwards it's a slippery slope toward one of two ends. Either you push yourself toward stress, anxiety, chronic fatigue and ever-increasing self-sabotage, or you emulate male energy to ensure your success, but other parts of your life suffer. Either way, it's utterly exhausting.

Now it's time to bring in the full understanding, the full enormity of the extent to which you have been undermined. You have been battling a mighty beast, while the world around you didn't see or acknowledge your efforts, your courage – didn't notice The Beast was there at all.

When you finally see what you've been up against, that feeling that there is something wrong with you can go in the bin. You have been basing your conclusions on flawed information; those conclusions are not valid.

Understand now that your subconscious has locked you into a battle to the death every day, and what is more, throughout that battle you have been stuck in a permanent state of zero power.

Take a moment. Feel that enormity.

It is a miracle that any of us have achieved what we have, and survived as long as we have.

EXERCISE: TAMING YOUR BEAST

You've got the theory, now for the practical. You're going to get to know your Beast, get to know it deeply and specifically. Knowledge is the first step to power, as we know. The more you understand The Beast, the more power you take back, and the smaller and more insignificant he will become.

1) How wounded am I?

Consider your life from birth to adulthood. Make a list of the situations, relationships and experiences that upset you, frightened you, humiliated you, or made you cry. I want you to include the big things, the little things and the ongoing things. If you have suffered any abuse of any sort, that counts. If you were bullied at school or lived in an environment where your parents' relationship was breaking down and they were shouting all the time, those things count. There's no right or wrong here, it's how you felt at the time that matters. It is your child's interpretation that defined your response, not your considered adult understanding.

Of course, you won't be able to remember everything, but you will remember the key events and experiences when you ask your mind to find them. If you still feel the heat of emotion – anger, fear, dread, humiliation – when you recall these memories, this is proof that you are still frozen and in submission. It's proof that part of your mind believes you are still there, that you're still in danger. This is true no matter how many decades have passed. Frozen means frozen.

2) How small is my power foundation?

It could be that you are a western woman who has been brought up with equality, rights and opportunities, or it could be that you are still oppressed by a patriarchal society or family. Underneath the surface, we will find the same thing. All of us are still carrying the energetic imprints, definitions and limitations of what women were expected to be in the past.

If you're a western woman, the best way of measuring your power foundation is to look at the lives of your grandmothers, or great-grandmothers. What was their highest level of education? What level of equality and opportunity (or lack thereof) did they experience? Did they work outside the home? If so, what did they do? Did they earn money or were they given the 'housekeeping' money by their husbands? What do you think was the limit of their aspirations?

If you are from a culture where women don't yet enjoy equality with men, your task is easier. Ask yourself, what is the 'perfect' behaviour, attitude, occupation, level of freedom and choice for a good, traditional, dutiful woman from your community?

These old-fashioned limitations are more or less what your subconscious thinks you should be doing in your life. I'm sure you are appalled at the idea of being limited in this way when you want and are capable of so much more.

3) Where am I going with my life?

Having found your subconscious benchmark of womanhood, it's time to identify just how far you have fought your way beyond it, into pioneer territory. Now let's analyse your own life, all aspects of it.

How much education have you received, or are intending to receive? Have you lived away from home, unmarried? Have you had sexual relationships outside of marriage? Do you work outside the home, and if you do, what is your career? How much authority do you have? Are you in a position of authority over men? Have you chosen not to have children and devote yourself to your career? Have you equalled or surpassed any of the men in your family? How much money do you earn, and how much do you intend to earn in the future? Do you stand up to the men in your life?

If you are still being controlled and oppressed because of your family, nationality or culture, then instead of analysing what you are doing now, consider what you would *choose*, if you had the freedom. The fact that other women in the world have freedom means that you too will desire it, a key point.

4) Spot the difference.

I expect your life, dreams, goals and aspirations are a million miles away from the traditional definitions of womanhood that your subconscious is clinging to so desperately.

This is your 'aha' or maybe your 'oh my goodness' moment. Take a few minutes and allow the enormity of the gulf between the old limits, and the life you want, to sink in.

This gulf creates huge internal conflict. Your subconscious mind wants you to obey the old rules; it knows the direction you should be going in and, when you stray from the path, it will try to bring you back, kicking and screaming if necessary.

Your conscious self is heading in a completely different direction; the direction of freedom, opportunity and doing exactly what you want with your life. The greater the divergence between these two paths, the greater the internal stress. Stress creates strain; strain is the amount something is stretched. You don't need to be a materials scientist like me to understand that you can only stretch something so far before it breaks.

This is precisely the process that is going on in your mind. The further you have moved from the traditional definitions, the more strain is put on your mind and body, and the more conflict will be created as a result.

This is your unique beast and you are now in a position to start taming it. Tame The Beast and you can start reversing that downward spiral of doom we talked about at the beginning.

12
Key Two: Compassion

One thing was clear: the world really wasn't on her side. The only person on her side, in this journey, was Grace herself.

But wait... was it really?

Grace took a long, hard look at herself. If she was honest, she wasn't on her own side either. From childhood she had done nothing but put herself down, tell herself she wasn't trying hard enough, that she wasn't good enough, that she was unattractive and not worthy of being liked, that she didn't really deserve success. She had always been her own worst critic – just like her mother and her grandmother before her.

How could she expect the world to treat her fairly if she couldn't even do it herself? But how could she stop criticising herself? Grace simply didn't have a clue.

Stop the self-criticism

Now that you have met your Beast, it is time to start your journey back to true power. It's time to activate the second key to female empowerment: *Compassion.*

Nearly all women have a default response of harsh self-judgement, attributing everything that isn't perfect to a personal failure. We are brilliant at bringing ourselves down; this is our Achilles' heel. While the default male response is to blame external factors for things that aren't going right, or chalk it up to a lesson learnt, the default female response is to assume personal inadequacy and beat ourselves up. While we stay in this mindset, we do a brilliant job of making everything worse.

As if this weren't enough, we have an added problem: women aren't 'meant' to look after themselves. Deep in our ancestry are longstanding patterns of self-sacrifice, putting everyone else first, and ignoring our own needs. The result is that most women feel deeply guilty every time they are kind to themselves. Put these two things together, and it's no wonder that we spiral into destructive self-judgement at the drop of a hat. These patterns are so entrenched that they are almost our identity.

Before we can turn things around, we must change our attitude toward ourselves. This can be done with many painstaking hours of reprogramming the subconscious mind, but we need something quicker; something that will loosen up those self-destructive tendencies and allow your energy to shift now. This is where compassion comes in.

What you have been through in your life, both the direct experiences and the underlying negative energies you now know about, leaves a harsh imprint on your mind, body and energy field. This includes the feminine wounds I talked about earlier, as well as lesser and ongoing challenges. These unresolved experiences get stuck as energy patterns within you and create limiting beliefs, keep you in energetic submission, eat away at your wellbeing, and undermine you at various levels.

To move forward, you need to acknowledge what you have gone through, allow yourself to feel the things you have suppressed, and give yourself credit for having coped with so much. You need to give yourself the gift of compassion.

If you are like me and have a 'fix it' mentality to personal development, you might well resist this step. Trust me, I resisted too, for a long time. I thought that by clearing, reprogramming, releasing and updating, I could sort everything out. I was wrong. The wounded parts of you will continue to create problems until they are truly acknowledged. Until your wounds are given the attention they need and demand, you won't get past them. Things will get worse. Uncomfortable though it is, this is an essential step that must be followed if you want to transform your life and embrace your true power.

When Female History Syndrome kicks in, you will doubtless start judging yourself harshly for having such a ridiculously out of proportion reaction. This self-judgement will exacerbate the problem. However, when you made those judgements, you had no idea what Female History Syndrome was. You had no idea that everything you wanted to do and be was labelled as forbidden, with the subheading of a death sentence. You had no idea that everything you chose to do was causing your subconscious to freak out and trigger your survival mechanisms. You had no idea that you were trying to fit yourself into a patriarchy box where only male is acceptable, making everything you did an instant failure. Need I go on?

To put it another way, you thought you were running away from a small dog that everybody else thought was cute. In reality, there was also a huge, hungry grizzly bear chasing you. You couldn't see it, but you could feel it. Your reaction was not at all out of proportion. Now you know, so everything is different. What you need is a huge dose of understanding, compassion, kindness and acknowledgement – you are more than entitled to it.[9]

---

9   If you have gone through serious trauma and abuse, I would strongly advise you to seek help to resolve these experiences, as you will need support working through them.

Mirror, mirror on the wall

What can you do to let compassion in? There are different levels, and it's up to you how deep you want to go. The first step is conscious recognition. For this, you simply need to sit with your situation and your experiences quietly and allow yourself to feel. Feel what you have been through. Feel into the enormity of The Beast you have been battling. Allow those sensations, memories and understandings to be felt and acknowledged. This takes time, and uncomfortable feelings are likely to surface. In this context, it is healthy to cry, to feel anger, to feel whatever comes up for you. If you need to beat up a pillow, sob until your dripping mascara turns you into a panda or swear profusely, do it. I've done all these things. This is the self-acknowledgement you need.

It can also be helpful to journal. This is an effective way of processing your feelings. Remember, the goal is to release the judgement that there is anything wrong with you because of the way you have reacted to life. We are replacing every judgement with understanding and compassion.

I'm going to share with you my favourite way of releasing self-judgement and replacing it with compassion. It's simple, but the shift in mindset is beyond liberating.

EXERCISE: THE MAGIC MIRROR

Here is our challenge: as women, we are hardwired to criticise ourselves and set ourselves impossible standards that we'd never impose on anyone else. The solution? We switch positions with someone else.

You are now armed with the awareness of the true scope of your battles and challenges. You have got to know The Beast. Yet at this point, you are still subconsciously beating yourself up with a big stick, labelling yourself a failure and in doing so, blocking love, happiness, abundance and the nurturing your system desperately needs.

The magic mirror process

1. Look in your mirror. Look directly into your eyes, and hold this connection. Forget about what you look like. Ignore whether your hair is right or your makeup is done. Look beyond that superficial appearance. Look to your soul within.

2. After a minute or two, your brainwaves will begin to shift down toward the alpha frequency where you can access a meditative state.

3. Imagine that the person you are looking at is not you. She is a stranger who has lived your life. She has gone through everything you have, with every block, every bit of conditioning, every trauma and every symptom of Female History Syndrome you have.

4. In your mind, imagine that you have met by chance, and she tells you her story. That woman in the mirror isn't you. What you'll find is that your perspective immediately shifts away from

self-judgement. In this place, you can now access the natural compassion and understanding you would have for another person. This is where we can use our in-built advantage, our innate conditioning to be understanding and care for others.

5. Consider now every detail of her story. Look at how she has been treating and judging herself. Look at how out of proportion everything is. Not only has she been unbelievably harsh on herself for the way she has reacted, now you can see her beast undermining and attacking her at every turn. All this is happening while the world refuses to even acknowledge that beast.

6. When you have allowed the whole picture to sink in – this will take several minutes at least – imagine giving her the recognition, the kindness and the compassion she deserves for everything she has been through. Acknowledge her courage and determination. For some people, this process works best if you talk out loud. For others, it is more powerful in your head. There is no right or wrong way of doing this, it's just what works best for you.

We have spent our whole lives putting ourselves into the straitjacket of self-criticism, and you won't be able to get yourself out in one attempt. I recommend that you repeat this exercise whenever you become aware that you are treating yourself harshly. Just a few minutes will release that self-judgement and shift your mindset. By training yourself in this way, you will gradually undo the damage and create a new way of dealing with life.

Next-level compassion

Now I want to go deeper. I am always looking for a big transformation. If you are on that page too, this next step is for you. What we need to do is not only to feel and understand, but also to release those energy patterns that are sitting in our minds and the cellular memories of our bodies. All our experiences are held within our being as energies, and it is only when we lift those out that we feel free. I have included an audio version of this compassion meditation in the online resources to accompany this book, but here is the process set out for you to follow.

EXERCISE: THE COMPASSION MEDITATION

I recommend spending at least twenty minutes doing this exercise.

1. Sit comfortably. Relax and close your eyes. Breathe gently, and as you do so, imagine yourself breathing in a beautiful coral sparkly light. With each breath in, feel the energy filling your lungs and sinking into your cells. Feel it growing stronger, soaking into your heart and flowing around your body. It feels so soft and safe that you can allow your mind and body to let go of the stress and tension of your day. Let yourself simply float in the coral energy.

2. As you imagine the coral energy filling your mind and body, feel it flowing up through your chest, out of the top of your head, then down the outside of your body, and back up through your feet. This is

an ongoing circulation of energy that follows the natural electromagnetic field created by your heart.

3. Once you are in this relaxed state, you are ready to start releasing and healing yourself. Allow your memories and understandings of your life to come into your mind, and see each one as an energy pattern. These patterns have served their purpose and now you can release them. Simply imagine the coral energy washing over them and gently dissolving those patterns.

4. Just be with this energy, and allow your mind and body to process what's happening as the old patterns are released. Stay in this state as long as you wish.

When you are ready to come back, gradually become aware of your body, move your hands and feet, and then open your eyes. It is a good idea to eat and drink something after doing this exercise as you will need to ground yourself before you carry on with your day.

It's important to understand that this meditation isn't something you need to try hard at; this is something you just allow to happen. I know the concept can be challenging for focused individuals like myself, but if you try to force it you'll meet resistance. Let go of the control and simply let the patterns release as you gently rest your attention on each feeling and memory.

As with the magic mirror exercise, the compassion meditation isn't something you will only do once. It is an ongoing process of acknowledgement and healing which will take considerable time. Long sessions doing this meditation are not necessary – what is important is to do it regularly. By bringing in these frequencies of compassion you can loosen and shift a lifetime of self-judgement and criticism. This is immensely powerful for unlocking negativity and opening up the new possibilities of empowerment and wellbeing you have been seeking.

13
Key Three: Power

'Why have I been obeying all these ridiculous rules?' thought Grace to herself.

Good question! Now that she looked at the situation, it seemed ridiculous. Why hadn't she stood up for herself? Why hadn't she said no? Why hadn't she shouted or refused or just done what she wanted and ignored everyone else?

Why hadn't she taken her spell book out earlier – not just earlier today, but years ago?

Reversing the submission response

Now we've reached the exciting bit. This is the key that changes everything. The first two keys paved the way, now you are ready for the game-changer: *Power*.

We understand now that Female History Syndrome, combined with our own life experiences, creates the subconscious misperception that we are in extreme danger. This triggers the submission response, leaving us powerless, which in turn makes us feel even less safe, and locks us into a perpetual fight or flight mode.

My Pull Back Your Power technique allows you to reverse your submission response and, in doing so, can change your life. Changing your subconscious beliefs and learning assertive body language will not affect how you feel underneath, while you are locked into energetic submission. Logically, the only way for you to feel better, and for your body and mind to switch off the danger response, is to get your power back.

In this section, you will learn how to do precisely this. You can take this process deeper with me if you want a more profound transformation, but if you follow the instructions given here, you will feel a tangible shift in your interactions with other people and the world.

Identify your submission triggers

When I have introduced women to the idea that they have been spending their lives in submission, this invariably provokes resistance and even anger. I completely understand why. We are modern women and do not want to believe we are going into submission, like some dutiful, demure, downcast sixteenth-century serving girl. Trust me, I was just as horrified when I realised that I was doing it. I was even more horrified when I realised that years of clearing my traumas and reprogramming my subconscious mind, had in no way ameliorated my submission response. I was still as energetically submissive as I had ever been.

It's important to come out of denial and establish whether you are indeed spending your life in submission. This is simple to identify, and you should already have done this exercise in the 'What Is Power?' chapter. If you didn't, make sure you do before continuing. You need to know the situations that trigger your submission response so you can pull back your power.

To quickly recap, if you experience any of the following symptoms, this is indicative of a submissive state. Try to become aware of which are most dominant for you, and the situations or relationships that most commonly send you into submission. The symptoms are:

- Anxiety, fear, panic or dread

- Stress

- Worry, dwelling on something, or over-analysing

- Feelings of hopelessness, despair or depression

- Inability to open your mouth and express your opinion even though you want to

- Chronic exhaustion, insomnia, or conditions such as IBS, fibromyalgia, migraines and other ongoing ailments

- 'Butterflies' in the stomach or a sinking feeling in the gut

- Feeling not good enough

- Feeling that anything less than perfection is failure

- Any form of self-harm

- Any eating disorder or fixation with body image

- Any form of compulsive self-comforting behaviour (eating, shopping, substance abuse, alcohol etc)

- Anger and aggression, using 'fight' as motivation

- Lashing out, verbally or physically, toward yourself or others

- Any rejection of your femininity, labelling the 'soft' female way as weak and inferior, or need to emulate archetypal male energy and behaviour

Every time you experience any of the above, you have most likely gone into energetic submission and are running on zero power.

When I became aware of this deep level of energy flow in human interactions and realised why simply changing beliefs wasn't making any difference to the way I felt, I started to monitor what I was doing on an energetic level as I went through my day. I became aware of what my energy did as I spoke to people, worked on projects, relaxed, and how this correlated with how stressed or anxious I felt. The results were astounding. I discovered that I was living my life in a pretty constant state of submission and that any interaction of any kind, with any person (even those interactions I perceived as positive) resulted in me allowing my power to drain away completely.

This blew me away.

I immediately started investigating how I could stop doing this. Nothing had ever been more essential for my wellbeing. The technique I discovered was not only quick and easy, but it could also be taught to anyone. You don't need to be a healer, you don't need any special abilities. It simply uses the energetic connection we all have with the universe and the people around us.

The power of attention

At this point, I want to talk about the relationship between power and mental attention. It is a fact that attention magnifies power. Pure and simple. What you focus on, whether negative or positive, will magnify. As you activate the power key, you will realise how essential it is to understand this concept.

When you are in submission, your attention is completely locked on the other person or issue. You are putting all your focus outside of yourself and onto the object of your stress. In your mind, you think this is the best thing to do because it allows you to analyse the situation thoroughly and work out the best response. In short, you believe this will make you as safe or as successful as possible in that situation. You are deluding yourself. This logic is flawed, and it is making things worse.

Consider for a moment the African Serengeti. You are the zebra. Your world is full of danger – a lion, leopard or cheetah could leap out at any moment and rip out your throat. The only way to survive is to focus your attention outside yourself. You must be hyper-alert to any movement, cover all directions, and be prepared to flee for your life. All your focus must be on perceived danger, none of it on yourself. This is the only way you can survive.

This behaviour, deeply ingrained into our brains, is the behaviour of the weak; the animal with no power who is at the mercy of the strong. Putting your focus outside of yourself is screaming out this message loud and clear. When you do this, you are telling the people around you that you are their prey and they are the hunters. You are announcing your powerless state. You are playing the part of the hunted.

Then, because you are focusing all your attention on the external situation or person, you start to magnify that energy. If there is fear, you magnify it. If there is conflict, you magnify that. If there are programmes telling you that you are doing something forbidden for a woman and will be punished for it, those escalate. You soon become locked into a vicious energetic cycle that takes away your power, tells everyone else you are powerless, and magnifies all that negative energy. It couldn't be worse. Try as you might, once you are locked into this response, it feels practically impossible to drag yourself out of it. What we need is a new angle to deal with it and pull back your power.

Changing the power balance

Unfortunately, the submission response is locked into our physiology. The exact details of how you respond depend upon your experiences and the way you are compensating. (There is a specific response associated with each of the Female Power Archetypes, which is the subject of a future book.) You also can't yet change the entire matrix of human interaction and negate the energy flow of the patriarchal legacy – no matter how much you'd like to.

What you can do is change the power balance between you and the world, in the moment, and change how your body feels. When you give your body back its power, it starts to feel safe again, which in turn reduces stress responses. Result: your submission is reversed. This is the key to escaping that downward spiral we talked about, and it's the key to freeing yourself from Female History Syndrome.

I'm now going to introduce you to my Pull Back Your Power technique. This is simple, quick and easy, but utterly life-changing.

The status quo will always hold the energetic power, regardless of whether the official line has changed. Nothing will shift until we actively pull back our power.

EXERCISE: PULL BACK YOUR POWER TECHNIQUE

Imagine you are interacting with another person and you realise you have gone into submission. This is what to do:

1. Imagine a wire connecting your chest to the other person's chest. Threaded onto this wire is a large brightly coloured ball. This ball represents the power dynamic between the two of you, where the person with the ball has the power. To start with, the other person has the ball – they have all your power.

2. In your mind's eye, reach out and grasp the ball. Now pull it back, sliding it along the wire. Pull it right back and bring it into your chest. This can be more difficult than it sounds when you are stuck in submission. Sometimes I have had to pull again and again before I get the power back to me. This will take a good few seconds. It is not something you can do with a click of your fingers. It is a real pulling process and there will be some degree of resistance as you try to shift that power dynamic.

3. When you have brought the ball back to you, focus all your attention onto that ball, as you hold it within your chest. Focus, focus, focus. Don't leave any of your attention on the other person. This sounds easy, but it does take a conscious effort. At this point, you are undoing all that negative magnification and bringing back your power.

As you hold on to the ball and hold your focus on it, your power will increase. The longer you can hold this focus, the more effective the exercise will be. I have seen and measured the power increase in my clients as they hold this focus, and they invariably agree that they feel very different. This happens from the first time of using the technique.

It's as simple as that. Once you've got the hang of it, you can begin to use the technique everywhere in life where you have lost your power. You can pull back your power from past, present or future situations. You can use it to resolve issues, in relationships, and in situ when you feel yourself losing your power. With practice, you will be able to do it quickly and feel immediate results.

If you have experienced trauma, pull back your power from those experiences. Use this technique on every wounding experience. (The reason all the healing I had done on the traumas in my life hadn't freed me from these experiences was that I didn't yet have my power back. When I did reclaim my power, everything changed.) Use it for ongoing conflicts in your workplace or personal life. Pull back your power from the childhood bullies. Use it in any situation that causes you stress and worry. There are no limits to the situations from which you can pull back your power.

This is only the basic version of the exercise. You can make it even more powerful by adding in your heart energy – I have created an audio meditation to teach you how to do this, which you'll find on the online resources page.

When you start using the Pull Back Your Power technique, you are counteracting a deeply ingrained response which you have been repeating, probably for most of your life. This power-draining mechanism is your autopilot. It feels normal and comfortable, even though it undermines you in so many ways. So don't expect to do this exercise once and for your entire life to change instantaneously. That simply isn't going to happen. Just as it takes regular conscious action to create a new habit, when you start pulling back your power, you are training your mind, body and energy field to behave in a completely different way.

When I first started doing this, I found that I would pull my power back in, but then I would start to lose it almost immediately because the feeling of having that power was so deeply unfamiliar to me. Undeterred, I got into the habit of pulling it back every time I thought about it. Just like training a muscle, my energy system began to learn how to hold on to its power.

Shortly after I discovered how to pull back my power, my husband, who is a CEO, suggested that I go to an entrepreneurs' workshop run by one of his acquain-tances. My immediate response was a pang of anxiety in my stomach and I thought up excuses not go to, but I decided to use the event to test my new techniques in the field. I arrived early and, feeling somewhat queasy, I walked around the park. I didn't have to test myself to know that I had already given away all my power in the typical submission response I had lived with my whole life. I then focused on the day and used my techniques to pull back my power from the idea of the workshop, meeting strangers, being out of my comfort zone, and everything else I could think of. Within a couple of minutes, I felt completely different and was able to walk confidently into the meeting. Once inside, I had another wobble and so repeated the power-pulling.

The results? In that workshop, I found myself speaking up, asking questions and contributing, easily and effortlessly. And I wasn't having to screw up my courage to do it. I felt completely relaxed and confident. My reaction was so not Anne-like compared with how I would normally feel in such a situation. In that sense, my techniques were an unmitigated success, but that wasn't all. In the break we did a little networking – a situation which I'd usually avoid like the plague – and I decided, in light of my initial success, to take the bull by the horns and try again. I pulled my power back in again and joined a group of people chatting. Here's the astonishing thing. They immediately turned and started talking to me, whereas in the past I would have been invisible. They gave me their attention because I was holding the power, energetically. Several even commented on how relaxed and confident I was compared with how they felt. I wasn't someone different. I hadn't changed who I was, I wasn't acting or faking anything, I simply felt relaxed and confident and very much myself.

Holding my power hadn't only changed the way I felt in that situation, it had also changed the way people treated me and responded to me. It was that day that I realised I had discovered something game-changing, which would transform the lives of many women.

You now have the first three keys to female empowerment at your disposal, and I recommend you start using them immediately. If this is all you do, you will change the way you feel and react to life. You can use the first three keys by yourself and get excellent results. However, if you want more, if you are ready for real transformation, now is the time to start going deeper.

14
Key Four: Perfection

Grace looked at the suit of armour she was meant to put on. It was designed for a man at least twice her height and girth. She couldn't even lift the sword. Naturally, George's armour fitted him perfectly.

Thumbing quickly through her spell book, as if by magic, the perfect spell presented itself.

'A spell to downsize, feminise and reduce weight by a factor of ten, while adding a decorative motif – perfect! Let's make this armour exactly right for me,' she said.

Healing Female History Syndrome

With the first three keys, you have learnt how to get yourself out of energetic submission, and how to stop dragging yourself down into the vicious cycle of self-judgement. Just being able to do these things will give you a huge advantage in life. But now you are going to enter new territory. With the fourth key, you are going to start freeing yourself from the shackles of Female History Syndrome, and opening up your path to achievement without personal cost.

First, a quick summary of the response we need to deactivate:

1. We feel the 'perfection is male' and the 'forbidden' messages

2. We feel our lack of power foundation

3. Our subconscious mind perceives danger, and panics

4. We go into submission and give all our power away to the other person, situation or institution

5. We shut down our female power and try to force ourselves to be what is acceptable (as defined by that old operating system)

6. Either we go into invisibility mode, or...

7. We push harder while continuing to feel that we are in danger

8. The result is huge internal conflict, stress, anxiety, which undermines confidence and wellbeing

This is our automatic response to the current energies of the world. History is what it is. Its legacy, the programming and conditioning of society, will eventually catch up, but this process will take longer than we are prepared to wait. Women do not have the power foundation that men have, and we do not have a world created in our image and based on our energy. These facts cannot be changed instantaneously. Meanwhile, gifted women like us certainly aren't going to give up and return to the kitchen, and neither is it acceptable that we continue to be held back and undermined by archaic legacy energies.

Remember the iceberg of the subconscious mind? This analogy works with institutions and the group consciousness too. Though at the top level we are given equality, the bottom part is submerged in the belief that 'perfection is male' and all the rules and limits of patriarchy, forbidding us from being, doing and achieving what we want. While this energetic status quo persists, we will continue to receive messages that trigger our danger responses, which in turn trigger our stress, our anxiety, our lack of confidence and everything else that keeps us from our true brilliance.

Changing this energetic response is essential if we are to stop being undermined. This is not easy to achieve; these messages are hidden, deep and they are everywhere.

What we need is:

- A method of shielding ourselves from the negative effects of those energies

- A way of undoing the damage that compensating for our lack of power has done to us

- A way of creating our own power foundation

With the above, we can stop those old beliefs hurting us, and create a level playing field of power so we are free to do and be exactly what we wish. This is exactly what we will do now, starting with the fourth key to empowerment: *Perfection*.

Fact vs feeling – perception vs truth

What specifically are you reacting to when Female History Syndrome is triggered? It is not the facts of your situation. Your subconscious mind and body are reacting to old energetic imprints and patterns. These are obsolete. They are patterns in the fabric of the energy matrix around us, not facts of solid reality.

Here is a good way of thinking about it. Many years ago, I stayed overnight in a very old guesthouse. The room was clean, nicely decorated, modern and in every way a pleasant place to spend the night. However, unbeknownst to me, underneath the floor was a cellar, which had been sealed up long ago. The cellar was full of mould and the spores were seeping up through the floorboards, which resulted in me experiencing the worst allergic reaction of my life. Instead of my body receiving signals of safety, cleanliness and comfort from the room I was sleeping in, it picked up the presence of something else, something which did not belong and had been there for a long time. This triggered my body's invasion alerts and resulted in a terrible allergic reaction. Each spore carried the message of an old, mouldy, damp cellar, which caused my system to freak out even though I was not in the cellar, I was in a clean, dry room.

This is our current energetic situation. In our modern lives, we have the opportunity and freedom to be educated, to achieve what we want, but under the surface of our world, the mould of the past is seeping into our lives. Each spore carries messages of subservience, of being forbidden, being punished, being inferior, and all the disempowering beliefs and restrictions from the past. Our subconscious minds and bodies forget our present surroundings and instead have a knee-jerk reaction to those old patterns. The persecution of powerful women, and the deep restrictions imposed on us throughout history, sit within our bodies and deep in our minds, and trigger deep-rooted fears. All this happens within the blink of an eye when we are exposed to that energetic pattern.

These patterns from the past are real, but they lack substance because they are no longer valid in civilised, enlightened society. The stress reactions we struggle with are triggered instantaneously, without any conscious awareness, analysis or discernment, because they are responses to what we feel. To free ourselves, we need to remind ourselves that the room we are in is clean and modern, take an energetic antihistamine, and clean the cellar out as soon as we can. In other words, we need to understand, at a cellular level, that what we are feeling is not supported by the facts. We need to show our bodies that the energetic pattern is no longer attached to genuine danger and it's safe to ignore it. We need to understand the difference between fact and feeling. We need to find a way of showing our subconscious minds the difference between what it perceives from the energy, and the truth. At the moment, we are being fooled.

We need a new set of definitions to work with. While the 'perfect' standard is male, we will always fail, be inferior and be undermined. What we need is a quantum shift, a new paradigm where we do fit in.

To extend my guesthouse analogy, say that all the rooms have been decorated in Art Deco style since the 1930s. Every five years, the rooms get a lick of paint and new soft furnishings, but always in the same style. Then I take over the guesthouse, decide I prefer the Scandinavian minimalist style and redecorate the whole hotel. If by definition all guesthouses must be Art Deco in style, I have ruined my hotel. But the newly decorated rooms fulfil every single requirement of a comfortable room, they are simply a different style. Our society is energetically stuck in the style of 'perfection is male' and this is recreated over and over again. Then we come in – modern, motivated, intelligent women – with a completely new style. We need to redefine what a guesthouse is, what society is, and make it suit our taste.

Unfortunately, the default state of the human mind is resistant to change. Our automatic response is that 'the same is safe, anything different is dangerous and to be avoided.' This is the programming that keeps people locked into archaic traditions full of disempowerment, prejudice and limitation. In our journey to free ourselves and embrace our full power, drastic change is essential. When you feel the resistance arise – and you will – remind yourself that this is just the knee-jerk response to change, and does not serve you.

In the second stage of this process, you will be defining your version of 'perfect'. A perfection that is your version of female. This is the only standard you should measure yourself against. The truer you are to yourself, the more perfect you become.

Freedom from patriarchal conditioning

It is an appalling fact that our subconscious minds are, by default, still holding on to patriarchal beliefs. When I started working on all this, I was not surprised to find these beliefs programmed into the women I worked with from patriarchal cultures, but I was horrified to find that the same beliefs were still programmed into my own mind. I had not been brought up with these attitudes, and yet they were there in my subconscious mind – clear evidence that my subconscious operating system was still programmed with ancestral beliefs and attitudes. Trust me when I tell you that ghastly, sexist beliefs are within you, undermining you at every turn.

Here are a few examples:

- Women must obey men
- Men are cleverer than women
- Men own women's bodies
- Power is men's God-given right
- A woman's place is in the home
- A woman's purpose is to serve men
- Women must never outshine men
- God is male

You are allowed to fume with rage when you read these. I could go on at length, but you get the drift. The 'rules' and 'laws' that define the patriarchal right to control, which oppress and limit us, are underpinned by this type of belief, and they still prevail in the subconscious and the group consciousness.

Your first step is to free yourself from such limiting beliefs, and in the online resources I have provided you with a healing for subconscious reprogramming which will do exactly this. I strongly recommend you listen to it as soon as possible. Once you have done this, you can move to the next stage of freeing yourself from the 'perfection is male' energy.

EXERCISE: REDEFINING PERFECTION

The 'perfection is male' energy will undermine you most in your career and any situation where you are out, visibly in the world, but it is still relevant in your personal life. I would suggest doing this exercise separately for each aspect of your life to get the best results. I have also included an audio version in the online resources.

To redefine your perfection:

1. Relax, focus into your heart and breathe gently for a few moments. Imagine the energy flowing up through your heart, out of the top of your head, around your body and back up through your feet, gently circling. Now imagine your energy expanding out and feel or imagine your connection with the universe.

2. Think about the situation you want to transform (eg your work environment). Allow all the details to come into your mind: the people, the buildings, the ethos, the behaviour and the way people interact with each other. Allow all this information to come up and just feel into it, without analysing anything for a few moments.

3. Now you can begin to analyse. How does it feel? Is it accepting, welcoming and nurturing? Or is it aggressive, confrontational and high-pressure? Is this a place where you feel you can relax and be yourself? Do you feel accepted as the real you, or are you trying to change yourself to fit in?

4. Next, I want you to become aware of the historical legacy underpinning that environment, or occupation. This is easy to do. Simply take your mind back one, two, three generations and take a look at that same environment, or its nearest equivalent. Is it a place where only men are allowed? If women are allowed, what is their role? Are they given the same recognition as the men? You know the answers to these questions already. This is the energetic level definition of that environment, and this will be the manifestation of the 'perfection is male' paradigm.

5. It's time now for awareness. Your subconscious mind and body have been feeling that old definition, accepting it, and measuring yourself against it. You have been unwittingly assuming that this energy is the way things have to be. Don't judge yourself for this, it's an automatic response that we all have.

6. Now allow yourself to feel the gulf between that old legacy energy and the present facts, between those old definitions and your right to participate as an equal, as yourself. How big is that gap? The bigger the gap, the greater the inner conflict, the more things will be labelled as forbidden, and the more that sabotage will undermine you.

7. Those old rules are an illusion, an echo, cobwebs in the attic that need to be vacuumed away. That is all. They have no hold over you, your life, your choices, or your safety. None whatsoever. Hold this understanding and allow it to sink into your mind and body as deeply as you can. Don't be tempted to skip over this quickly. The deeper you can imprint this understanding into your body, the more powerful the transformation.

8. Now that you have let go of those obsolete energies, it's time to create something new for yourself. Take a few minutes to decide what your new reference will be. What would that place be like, if it were perfect for you? What would be your perfect way of interacting, creating, working, if you could access your unique genius? How would people's behaviour be different? Make this as detailed as possible.

9. Finally, allow what you've created to soak into your mind and body. This is your definition of perfection. This is your benchmark, and when you measure yourself against it, there is nothing wrong with you. It is the expression of who you are and the fulfilment of your gifts.

Once you have created this energy of your perfection, I want you to connect to it regularly. The more you do it, the more the new patterns will become part of who you are and will replace those old legacy energies. This is the key to releasing self-doubt, self-sabotage and impostor syndrome, and is the foundation upon which you can thrive.

15
Key Five: Expansion

Grace stood victorious, sword raised above her head. She felt wild exhilaration. She was doing it; she was proving her mettle on the field. She was the equal of every man here.

But then she looked around and instead of the applause she was expecting, a sea of stony faces confronted her. Boos and jeers rang out. 'How inappropriate!' 'What is she thinking?' 'Well that isn't very attractive is it?'

Grace faltered. Her sword dropped to the ground. Being confronted with such disapproval was daunting and made her feel a bit queasy. Perhaps it hadn't been such a good idea to win after all.

The crash

Now that you have redefined perfect, and redefined what is permissible, you are well on the way to transforming your interactions with the world and the stress response that those old energy patterns trigger. When you have reached this point, you will be feeling a new optimism and things will begin to flow for a while. It is at this point that things tend to crash.

I am sure you will have experienced this phenomenon. You start to take action and push forward, expanding yourself, your business, or whatever you're striving for. Then you reach some invisible barrier and everything falls apart again. Typical occurrences are feeling blocked, fears and frustrations arising, procrastination, confrontation and conflict, avoidance and denial, illnesses, migraines, anxiety, and so on.

Does this sound familiar? It should, because it feels very much like our startling point. We might think that all our hard work has been for nothing and we've gone back to the beginning, but nothing could be further from the truth.

Here is our problem. Women are programmed with many limits. This is the 3D Spider's Web of Limitation in action. I use this analogy because it is such an evocative picture. Imagine yourself stuck in that web, pinned into position. Each time you try to move a limb, you are pulled back by the web. The more you push, the more you pull, the stronger the elastic force pulling you back to your original position. All those 'forbidden' labels are a multi-layered web that we are unable to get through.

We haven't gone back to the beginning, we have just reached the next level of programmed limitations. We don't have just one set of blocks to overcome when we start to expand into our potential, we have many. At each level, we will trigger a new layer of blocks, forbidden labels, and relative limits concerning the men in our lives, the traditional female roles, and the 'perfection is male' foundation of society. It's utterly frustrating, it's unfair, it's exhausting, but it is what it is. This is the world we have been born into, and this is the energetic system we need to overcome.

If we want to continue to move forward, we need to cut through these limits, over and over again. There is one way to do this, and that is *Expansion*, the fifth key to female empowerment. We must expand, and expand, and expand again.

Awareness, awareness, awareness

This is where you need your intellect and awareness on high alert. It is so easy to get stuck and give up as soon as the next level of blocks appear and start to pull you back down. Most women manage to do a bit of expansion, but then end up either pulling back or settling, because they don't understand what is happening or how to escape it.

Here's the essential point; every time you allow those old energies to stop you from doing and being what you want, you are letting the patriarchy win by keeping you small. When you let patriarchy win, you are intrinsically agreeing with those archaic beliefs that it is right for men to have the superiority and for us simply to serve. I don't know about you, but I will never allow that to happen. I know it is hard to push forward. It does require perseverance, courage, strength and determination, but the alternative is to acquiesce to the obsolete illusion of those old rules, and I will never do this. If you're reading this book, then it's more than likely you feel the same way.

The bottom line? It's vital that you have in place a clear procedure for dealing with these limits, and a primed awareness that prevents you from inadvertently falling back into subservience.

EXERCISE: ESCAPING THE WEB OF LIMITATION

To get through the layers of limitations you'll need to use all the skills and understanding you've learnt so far. I'll explain the thought process in steps here, and going through these carefully each time you feel a limit has been triggered will help you to free yourself. In many ways, this is a similar process to clearing the 'perfection is male' belief, but it takes things to the next level. For a deeper release, use the expansion clearing meditation in the online resources page.

To free yourself from limits:

1. Relax, focus into your heart and breathe gently for a few moments. Imagine the energy circulating up and

around your body as before. Then, pull back your power from the situation, using the ball visualisation from earlier.

2. Bring in the awareness that you have hit a limit and that the patriarchal legacy is trying to stop you from being, doing and having the things you want in your life. You feel the way you do, not because you aren't good enough, but because you have come so far. Acknowledge your success.

3. Try to identify what the limit is. Where in your life are you expanding beyond what is permitted? Remember that this can be an absolute limit (eg being in authority over men is forbidden for a woman) or a relative limit (eg earning more than my husband is forbidden). Remember that these definitions are most likely centuries old and that everything beyond a subservient, domestic role for women will likely be labelled as forbidden

4. Remind yourself that these rules are obsolete. You are 100% entitled to have any career you choose, to launch your business, and to be more successful than any man, whether that be a partner, brother or colleague. The law supports you in this. Any subconscious belief that you are breaking the rules by wanting these things for yourself is wrong.

5. Sit with this understanding. In your subconscious, programmes will be triggered that tell your body you'll be punished, tortured or put to death as a consequence of breaking the rules. You will not be put to death. Your subconscious is stuck in its ancient conditioning and doesn't realise that you are safe. By shining the harsh light of reality here, we see these old patterns for the illusions they really are.

6. Remind yourself (and you can smile at this if you wish) that when you outshine a man or succeed in a traditionally male career, you will not cause universal impotence in the male population, the earth will still keep orbiting the sun, the men won't all suddenly cease to exist. I know these things sound beyond ludicrous, but my years of plumbing the depths of the subconscious have found precisely these programmes holding women back again and again.

7. Remind yourself that you have reacted to energetic patterns which are no longer valid. It is my experience that we often react to someone's ancestral programming, instead of what they actually think. Nobody can be blamed for the ancestral programmes they have inherited. Often, these people are doing their best to fight against those patterns too; they don't believe them and don't act them out in their lives. If you asked the people in question, you would probably get an answer that is the opposite to the conclusion your subconscious mind has drawn. It's the facts that matter, not the energetic feeling, because the feeling is no longer based on reality.

8. Remind yourself that holding yourself back to stop someone else feeling inadequate or inferior is destructive. First, the world will be poorer if you stop yourself from contributing and creating everything of which you are capable. Second, when you bring your vibration down by blocking yourself, you drag others down with you. The only way to make the world a better place is for you to hold the highest possible vibration, this generates abundance

and positivity, which benefit other people. Anyone who finds their self-respect by holding women back, especially a woman they claim to love, has some big life lessons to learn about ego and human rights. Instead of pandering to their inadequacy, we should be helping them to evolve past these limiting attitudes.

9. This final stage is a very important one. Now we are going create a foundation to make your new patterning more robust. Imagine your current rights and entitlements extending backwards in time. Feel those rights belonging to your mother, your grandmothers, your great grandmothers, extending back into your ancestry. Mentally anchor this in place. Doing so will begin to create the idea of a female power foundation in your subconscious mind.

Constant vigilance

You must understand that this process of moving forward and then being blocked by new limits will happen repeatedly. Each time you expand, another layer of old limitations will be triggered. These can come from your childhood conditioning, your ancestry, your partner's ancestry, the group consciousness, and the subconscious programming of people around you. The key to increasing your success is to understand what is happening and why, and then push through those limits, never giving up.

We are the pioneers because we are the first women in history to have both the freedom and opportunity to fully express our talents in the world. The old energetic structures have not caught up with us, so we are entering new energetic territory. Pioneers always face challenge and struggle, but as each of us pushes through those energetic limits and releases those straitjackets, the group energy is shifted a little more, making it easier for all those who come after us. I know this can be small comfort when our lives are full of anxiety, blocks and burnout, but the truth is that this is the struggle of all women, and our efforts make a difference beyond our own lives.

16
Key Six: Mastery

Grace had thought this was a victory she only had to win once, but now she realised it wasn't that simple. There would be many challenges, many victories to win and much disapproval to ignore. This was her choice. Either go back to the corset, the straitjacket, and be a 'proper woman', or accept the endless obstacles, the disapproval and the backlash she had just gone through, but be her true self.

It didn't take long to make her decision. She was now the Sorceress and she was never going to turn back. Even knowing the cost, knowing that she would need to find that strength and courage again and again, there was no way she could return to being obedient and restrained.

Grace set her resolve and raised her sword again.

Being the Sorceress

Mastery of your true female power is an ongoing journey; in many ways, it is a journey of discovery. The longer you work with the first five keys to empowerment, the more you will open up the possibility of activating and embracing your true power. All the techniques and understandings you have learnt so far are designed to free you from the debilitating conditioning and limitations of the past and support you by beginning to create your power foundation. These do not, however, activate your true power.

By this point, you will understand that women have been stuck in the prison of patriarchy, which both limited what they can do, forced them to emulate the male way if they have any power at all, and shut down their unique powers. This shutting down of our true power is something that women have been forced to do for millennia. This pattern is ingrained in the group consciousness and our subconscious minds, and is reinforced by our wounding experiences. The result is that we are no longer aware of what our true powers are.

When I first started actively trying to open up my true powers, back in the days before I had discovered any of my power techniques, I was blocked again and again by huge fears. Each time I tried something, be it a simple guided visualisation or an exercise to open up my third eye, terrible anxieties and often a full-blown panic attack would result. It was not until I had spent many years freeing myself from historical and ancestral blocks that those abilities began to flow for me. I believe this phenomenon is typical. The ingrained conditioning that we 'must never go there again' kicks in and shuts the door firmly, even when we have only opened it a crack.

You have amazing powers of which you currently have little or no knowledge. Those that you are aware of are likely being blocked and sabotaged, and your true potential will be many times what you are currently experiencing. The sixth key to female empowerment is the discovery, activation and embracing of those powers. This is the stage where you step into your unique Sorceress.

Living the new paradigm

A new paradigm is needed. Each of us has lived our lives according to the 'perfection is male' paradigm and has unknowingly squashed ourselves into that box. While we have the mindset and outlook that this is the way things have to be, we will forever be shutting down our powers instead of letting them blossom.

From this point onwards, we must ditch the old paradigm and shift our mindset to the new. Our new paradigm is that every aspect of who we are, and what we can be, is completely valid and we are entitled to express it in the world, immediately. This makes us pioneers. We know we are going to meet resistance from the status quo, and in doing so trigger the men around us. It is inevitable and it is challenging. However, now that we understand the personal cost of *not* doing it, we cannot turn back. We are the trailblazers.

Your baseline understanding has to be that resistance from the status quo, although troublesome, is irrelevant. Becoming aware of the ways in which you are dumbing yourself down to fit in is essential. These automatic responses will have been programmed into your mind and body from childhood, as natural as breathing, whereas allowing yourself to relax into yourself feels deeply unsafe and alien.

Until you have done the preliminary work with the earlier keys, it will be practically impossible to move to this stage and retain your wellbeing. Once you have prepared the way, it all becomes possible. You must retrain yourself through awareness and repetition. As your power grows, you will feel safer doing this. Now you are in an upward spiral of growth instead of the downward spiral of disempowerment. You have the tools, the understanding and the power you need to realise your potential.

Discovering your powers

What are your powers? This is something you need to discover for yourself, all I will advise you is to release any limiting beliefs on what is or isn't possible. Your powers might be intuitive, psychic, and alchemical – nobody was more surprised than me when I discovered I had these things within me. They might be healing, inspirational or transformational abilities. They might be creative, through art, music or words. There is no limit once you free yourself from the paradigm of limitation and male perfection.

Your powers may lie in a field that was traditionally male-dominated, such as science, medicine, law, politics or business. It isn't that we stop doing these things when we embrace our full power – far from it. We are going to transform those fields. If you have excelled but suffered because of your lack of power foundation and the patriarchal status quo, then most likely you have achieved only a fraction of what you are capable of. You haven't found your true genius because you haven't brought all your abilities into play.

Imagine the world is an orchestra, but at the moment, instead of the full set of instruments, it only has a woodwind section (flute, clarinet, oboe and bassoon). Let's say those woodwind instruments represent the traditional male way of doing things. Perfection is male, so that was all that was considered necessary. The sections of the orchestra which represent the female way are missing. As a woman, you are handed the oboe part to play, because in this orchestra there are only woodwind parts. However, not being male, you don't have an oboe. Instead, you have a cello – a completely different instrument with a different technique, tone, range and sound. You can do your best to play the oboe part on your cello. You can read the music and have a good go at it, but you are going to find it much harder than someone with an actual oboe. What is more, you will always feel that mismatch, that the instrument you are playing, and the music you've been given, just don't align.

In our new paradigm, you hand back the oboe music and insist on being given a cello part. Once we have the correct music, everything fits into place and we can get the most out of our instrument. We don't have to adapt and compromise, instead, we can let the true beauty of the cello blossom through the music that was written for it. We are playing the same composition as the oboe, and we can play together, but our unique melody is now making the whole much richer than it was.

While we are subconsciously trying to squeeze ourselves into the patriarchy box, and crush the parts of ourselves that don't fit the old paradigm, we can only ever be and achieve a fraction of what is possible for us. It is not until we reject that box that we can fulfil our potential and transform the world in the process. It is those environments, careers and situations that are still heavy with 'perfection is male' energies that need us most.

Magnifying your power

When you are at this stage of blossoming, you will be following the empowerment keys as a way of life, pushing through limits, and bringing in all the awareness you have learnt so that the old subconscious manipulations no longer have power over you. Now is the time to magnify all your unique female powers intentionally, and you can do this in small yet significant ways that will help you tip the scale in your favour. To blossom, do everything you can to magnify your power and your feeling of safety in that empowerment, then actively allow your unique powers to develop.

This is the time to engage in female networking groups and join female masterminds. First, this diminishes the message that 'perfection is male' that you are inevitably still receiving from everyone around you. Second, it magnifies female energy and this has a profound effect on your subconscious mind by making you feel stronger and less likely to go into submission and undo all your good work. Third, on a conscious level, this allows you to start interacting in ways that are conducive to female nurturing and success. It's well established that women achieve more when helping and supporting each other, rather than following the competitive male model. If you're a woman trying to achieve success for herself out in the world, more than likely you have not yet experienced the female way as it *can* be.

A word of warning, though: remember that the women you interact with may still be bound by the old limitations, conditioning and wounded female energy, enacting one archetype or another – they are still undermined by Female History Syndrome. What you want to avoid is being dragged back into any of those compensation mindsets and power dynamics. By going on your power journey, you have freed yourself from the need to do things that way, and have completely changed how you interact with the world. When you are part of other women's groups, always keep that at the back of your mind. You are now the Sorceress archetype and have a completely different understanding and outlook on your power and your relationship with the world. Make sure you remain the pioneer and don't plug back into the old ways. Even better, join a community where the women are on board with the Six Keys to Empowerment. This will make things much easier for you.

If you are from a culture or family that is still actively patriarchal and that does not promote women's freedom, try to get to know women from more liberal backgrounds. Each time you engage with someone whose baseline programming is more empowered, it will have a beneficial knock-on effect for you and will not only help your own shift toward power but also help all the other women in your family and community.

Our bottom line, regardless of our background, is that we have the right to choose what our lives look like, to choose our professions, to be treated as equals. Any beliefs that say otherwise are obsolete and unjustifiable, and anyone who says otherwise is doing so to stay in a position of authority so they can oppress us. They do not have that right.

Reawakening your female powers

All you need to do is be open and receptive. When the restrictions and fear-based limitations are removed, you will naturally begin to blossom. The natural state for humanity is expansion and growth. It is an effort to hold back. To expand is the natural expression of who we are and is not something that needs to be forced. When your mind feels the freedom you have been seeking, your suppressed powers will begin to reassert themselves. You will have opened the doors to allow the true you to step out and the universe to show you the next steps. Release all attachment to the outcome – and believe me, I know that is easier said than done. By deciding in advance what we can have, do and be, that in itself places limits on what life can bring us. When we let that go and allow a more organic process to occur, miracles happen.

A goal-orientated approach, while useful for achieving specific things, is the male way, and the way in which anyone with a western education is trained and conditioned. We aren't rejecting it. Instead, we are introducing the 'wild card' of our unique female brilliance. Take on the mindset that your brilliance and power is a fact and allow that fact to shine, even if tentatively at first. The vibration this creates within the energetic matrix around you will not only feed your progress, but it will also inspire and attract different experiences in your life.

It's crucial to be constantly vigilant. Those pesky patriarchal limits and conditioning will continue to trigger as you expand further and further. If you aren't careful, you could fall back into their trap and find yourself pulling back and suppressing your power again. As long as you understand the triggering process, are always alert to anxiety and feeling blocked, recognise these as signs of a limit and use the tools you've been given, you will push forward to the next level.

We now have tools that women have never had before; tools which can undo energetic inequalities and allow us to take our rightful place safely. It's up to us to use them to help not only ourselves but all women. Using those tools will take you further than you ever believed possible, and will gradually train your mind and body to hold your power. When this energetic state feels safe and normal for you, magic will happen in your life.

When you step into your Sorceress archetype, you activate your greatest power, align with your true self and live in your genius zone. This is where profound confidence flows and soaring success can be yours. This is now possible for you.

17

Your Power Foundation Rituals

'The Sorceress Spell Book'

Chapter 1 – Activating Your Female Alchemy Powers
Chapter 2 – Vanquishing Demons
Chapter 3 – Advanced Beast Taming
Chapter 4 – Magical Business Tools
Chapter 5 – Conjuring Your Cloak of Safety and Credibility'

'Perfect,' said Grace to herself. 'What need have I for a sword and armour now?'

Developing your power foundation

In this final section, I give you quick and simple procedures that you can start using right away to develop and consolidate your power foundation. These are meant to be used alongside the deeper transformational exercises I've given you in the Six Keys chapters. I've designed them to fit easily into your normal life. It's frequency that matters, not the amount of time you spend doing them.

Your goal is to:

- Feel less anxious and more confident every day
- Train your energy field to hold your power instead of letting it slip away
- Find new ways of dealing with life's challenges

When you do these things regularly, you will feel more powerful, more confident and more in control. You will also be sending out a different energetic message to the people around you and this will inspire different reactions.

EXERCISE: MORNING POWER

This exercise will set your energy and power for the day. I recommend doing this in the shower so it becomes an indelible part of your daily routine.

1. Take a few slow breaths, close your eyes and focus into your heart.
2. Then, on an in-breath, imagine pulling back your power from the world and see, feel or visualise it flowing back into your chest. Hold your breath for a few seconds as you imagine the power anchoring in place. Mentally hold the power there. This step will,

over time, retrain your energy to behave differently. Remind yourself that this power state is now your default.

3. Now cast your mind over your schedule for the day. Become aware of anything you will be doing that might have a 'forbidden for women' label or a 'this is too much, relative to someone else' label. Remind yourself that these labels are not based on the rules we now live by and see them for what they are, illusions. Imagine those labels all disappearing. See yourself holding that power in every interaction and conversation, and see each task you perform as being entirely within your rights and entitlements.

4. Visualise the outcomes you want for the day.

EXERCISE: EVENING POWER

In the evening it is important to resolve and pull your power back from all the events of the day. Inevitably, you will be exposed to confrontation, stress and the unexpected. You will still come across situations and people that trigger you to give away your power and go into submission. By doing this exercise each evening, you will stop the accumulation of disempowerment in its tracks and continue your progress in pulling back your power.

1. Take a few slow breaths, close your eyes and focus into your heart.

2. Allow the events of the day to come into your mind. Identify anything which has caused symptoms of submission (anxiety, stress, holding back, anger, frustration) and every situation where you were not treated with full equality and respect.

3. Consciously pull back your power from each incident and each person involved. Do this using the 'ball on a wire' visualisation to make it most effective.

4. Hold the power in your chest, and bring your attention back from those events. If you have gone into submission, this can be hard and might take a minute or two. Keep at it until you have both got the ball back to your chest and brought your full attention back to your own body.

5. Focus your attention in your chest, holding your power, for a couple of minutes at least. The longer you do this, the more of your power will return and the better you will feel.

6. Remind yourself that the reasons you went into submission are not valid; it was a knee-jerk reaction to deep-seated conditioning. You don't need to obey these responses any longer.

EXERCISE: GATHERING YOUR POWER FOR A FUTURE EVENT

If you're anything like me, the amount of energy you can spend agonising about future events can be off the scale. Before you've got your power back, normal events frequently feel like ordeals to be survived and can suck the joy out of life. This is a deeply ingrained pattern for many women. Using this exercise, you can defuse this response and, over time, you will react less intensely to such events. If you have something particularly triggering coming up – for example, an interview, a presentation, an appraisal, an audition, a difficult conversation – repeat this exercise many times in the days leading up to it. The more you do it, the more empowered you will remain during the event.

Part A: In preparation

1. Take a few slow breaths, close your eyes and focus into your heart.

2. Analyse what this future event consists of. What are you going to be doing, being and experiencing? How do you want to behave? What outcome do you want?

3. Become aware of how much of this is labelled as 'forbidden for women' or 'this is too much relative to someone else'. Usually, most of what you want will be labelled in this way. It is this conflict between what you want to do, and your subconscious believing it will result in terrible punishment, that is the true cause of your anxiety or lack of confidence.

4. Remind yourself that you have reacted to obsolete subconscious conditioning – conditioning designed to keep us women small and subservient – and that we are not going to allow these rules to restrain us any longer.

5. Visualise or feel those 'forbidden' labels disappearing. It can be helpful to do this in an evocative way – imagine them being blown up, or incinerated, or dissolved with acid if you wish. Of course, if you want to see them transforming into light and love, that's fine too. Just get rid of those labels in a way that works for you. Replace them with labels of 'easy for me' and 'permitted'.

6. Pull back your power from that future event, and all the people and institutions involved. Focus on that power within your chest and away from anything else, to tip the power balance in your favour.

7. Repeat the above frequently in the days leading up to the event.

Part B: Just before the event itself

8. Take a few slow breaths and focus into your heart. *Do not* close your eyes.

9. Pull back your power from the event and the people there. Feel that power flowing back to you, and take a few moments to anchor it in place. When I do this it feels as if I am tensing a mental muscle and consciously holding it in place.

10. Tell yourself that it is your right to retain your power throughout the experience, and it is your right to shine and outshine as much as you wish to, without unpleasant consequences or reprisals. It is your right.

11. Take a deep breath and get on with what you have to do.

EXERCISE: DEALING WITH CONFRONTATION

We will, many times in our lives, come up against people (often, but not always, men) who, supported by their big power foundation, ego and personal agenda, will use their larger size, louder voice and probably wounded male energy to try and intimidate us and get their way. We've all experienced this in work situations, and sometimes in our personal lives. Such incidents are damaging to us because they trigger the childhood submission response. A nasty exchange like this can drain our power almost instantaneously and set us back.

Next time you find yourself in a confrontation:

1. Remind yourself that you are dealing with wounded male energy, and you are under no obligation to submit. Even someone who is your superior in a work hierarchy is obliged to treat you with consideration and courtesy.

2. Pull back your power. If you can't imagine the ball and wire while you are in the situation, imagine your body is like a magnet, and your power is attracted back to you like iron filings. Feel the energy of your power flowing back to you and, as it fills your body, you will feel yourself becoming more confident and less intimidated.

3. Mentally detach from the exchange and, instead, focus on your own body. This will magnify your power.

This procedure takes just a few seconds and, with practice, you can do it easily while still engaging in conversation. As you bring back your power, your adversary will feel less confident and the dynamic will shift noticeably. Doing this regularly can change the whole basis of your interactions.

Reclaiming your power from sexual harassment

The #metoo era has, thankfully, made people aware of just how much harassment women have to deal with daily. I could write at least another book on my experiences of this in the world of engineering. Whether we experience an actual assault or an ongoing undercurrent of harassment, it will undermine us profoundly if we don't get our power back. Why? Because not only are the incidents themselves nasty, they emphasise the message that a woman is only worth what her body can give a man. They dehumanise us and take away our power and our rights. No incident, no matter how small, is a woman being 'over-sensitive' or 'making a fuss about nothing', or 'lads just having fun'.

Identifying harassment is simple. When an incident occurs, if you have that sinking, nauseous feeling in your stomach, followed by a deep fury later, it has crossed the line and taken away your power. Dealing with the experience at an energetic level is essential, and when you have done so you will be in a much more powerful state and will have more clarity on the most appropriate action to take.

One more note here, in my years of empowering women, I have become expert in healing the subconscious and energetic effects of sexual assault and rape. Many women have gone years with the energetic effects of these experiences undermining their lives. In every case, when they come to me, they are still frozen in an energetic state of zero power – a severe feminine wound – even decades after the event. This is the case regardless of whether they had sought counselling or used other healing modalities.

Using my techniques to pull your power back from both the event, and the perpetrator, is a new step you can take towards your healing, and in my experience, can provide a quantum leap in getting your life back. While you are energetically frozen in zero power, the event will continue to have power over you. *I'm not saying that you use these techniques instead of seeking conventional help – far from it. Always consult your doctor and take whatever conventional help works for you.* Simply add pulling back your power to whatever actions you take. This will make you feel mentally stronger, help free you from fear and definitely help you to reclaim your life.

EXERCISE: DEALING WITH SEXUAL HARASSMENT

The purpose of this exercise is twofold: to cleanse the energy of the perpetrator from you, and to get your power back. This is how I recommend you proceed to get your power back from the experience:

1. Take a few slow breaths, close your eyes and focus into your heart. Imagine the energy flowing up through your heart, out of the top of your head, down the outside of your body and then back up through your feet. Stay with this cycle of energy for a few moments.

2. Breathe slowly and imagine the energy in your heart getting stronger and expanding.

3. You will have gone into total energetic submission, regardless of how big or small the incident was, and regardless of what physical action you took at the time. Before you can shift your understanding of and feelings on what has happened, you must get your power back. Use the 'ball on a wire' visualisation and actively pull your power back from both what has

happened and the person or people involved. This may take a while and you may need to do it several times.

4. When you have succeeded in getting it back, hold the ball of your power in your chest. Focus on that power and breathe slowly, feeling your power magnify and expand as you do so. Focus intently on yourself, and I mean intently. Feel your power growing and growing, and the presence of the perpetrator getting smaller and smaller.

5. When your power has fully returned, imagine the energy of the perpetrator leaving your mind, your body and your energy field and flowing back to where it came from. Everything associated with what happened flows away, leaving you clear, clean and uncontaminated by the incident. Imagine yourself becoming brighter and more sparkly as this happens.

6. Finally, reaffirm the truth of the situation. The perpetrator acted on base and archaic motivations which have no place in this day and age. They are 100% in the wrong, and you are utterly blameless. Nothing they do to you can in any way diminish your value; not your value as a human being, your intellect, your creativity, your identity or your contribution. Your value has nothing to do with what may have happened to your body, or any unenlightened man's beliefs. They are irrelevant. They are nothing. There is no need to switch to a Snow White archetypal response here. You are an empowered Sorceress and can use your power to deal with these experiences.

7. When you have done this healing exercise several times, you will have the power and clarity needed to take any real-world action you think is appropriate for you.

If you have experienced serious abuse or assault of any kind, you do need to seek help with transforming the experience. However, if you do this exercise as soon as you are able, and repeat it, you will reclaim your power and make it easier to do the big healing work.

What Will Your Story Be?

How will you continue your story? Women have never before had both the knowledge and the tools to free themselves from the historic legacy of female disempowerment. Now, you do.

Think about how much you have accomplished in your life up until now, while having to fight The Beast every single day. Imagine what you could do without The Beast dragging you back at every turn, and without the straitjacket of the Web of Limitations. There is no need to for you to continue being undermined by subconscious submission, obsolete forbidden labels and the 'perfection is male' programming of our world. You can create a genuine power foundation for yourself, where your mind and body feel safe and the playing field is finally level. It's up to you and me, the female pioneers at this key point in history, to create that new energetic paradigm which will enable all women to thrive.

Use the tools I've given you. Pull back your power. Reactivate your brilliance. Reject the patriarchy box and step into your limelight – the boardroom, the conference hall or the world stage.

Enough is enough. Now is our time. Are you ready?

Grace closed her eyes. She felt her power reawakening. She smiled a secret smile. How silly she had been all this time, allowing herself to be ordered about, undermined and sabotaged by those stupid rules. She knew she was powerful enough to ignore them. She was ready. She pointed her hand at the obstacles on the field in front of her. Blinding violet light shot forth and disintegrated the whole lot.

'Much better!'

And now for that pesky Beast!

Grace turned back towards the place where, up until mere moments ago, The Beast had been lurking. Where was he? She looked more closely. There he was, standing on the lawn, the neatly mowed blades of grass reaching up to his neck. In the exact same moment that she had unleashed her true power, he had shrunk and was now only a few inches tall. He now looked very surprised, and quite cute, she decided.

George was struggling with his suit of armour and his broadsword. As the violet light flooded the field, he started in shock and promptly fell over. He did look rather silly, Grace thought, but quite sweet nonetheless. She looked at the other men; how dare they have treated her so appallingly? She could take her revenge now. She could make them suffer for what they had done, turn them into frogs maybe.

What would be the point, though? That would make her no better than them. She was better than them – a lot better.

'Hey, George,' she called, 'Why don't we forget this stupid contest? I have no desire to defeat you. There's room for us both in the Palace of Success.'

But George wasn't listening. He, the King and all the other men were looking at Grace as if seeing her for the first time. She saw respect, even awe, in their faces. The faces of the women in the crowd showed something else entirely: delight, and a realisation that perhaps they could do this too.

'Excellent,' thought Grace to herself, unable to hide the broad grin that was spreading over her face. 'What shall I do now, I wonder?'

Here begins the story of Grace the Magnificent!

The Beast always was an illusion, an echo of times past. Our subconscious minds just didn't realise this and behaved as if The Beast were real. When we have pulled back our power, and released that obsolete conditioning, we see that there is no beast, just us, in our brilliance and power.

To get started on your journey scan the QR code below or visit www.feminineconfidence.com/pullbackyourpowerbonuses to access bonus audio meditations and clearings to help you with each of the Six Keys to Empowerment.

Bibliography

Babcock, Linda, and Laschever, Sara, *Why Women Don't Ask: The high cost of avoiding negotiation, and positive strategies for change* (Piatkus Books, 2008).

Criado Perez, Caroline, *Invisible Women: Exposing data bias in a world designed for men* (Chatto & Windus, 2019).

Gleadle, Kathryn, *British Women in the Nineteenth Century* (Palgrave, 2001).

Hendricks, Gay, *The Big Leap: Conquer your hidden fear and take life to the next level* (HarperOne, 2010).

Kay, Katty, and Shipman, Claire, *The Confidence Code: The science and art of self-assurance – what women should know* (HarperCollins, 2014).

McTaggart, Lynne, *The Field: The quest for the secret force of the universe* (Element, 2003).

Acknowledgements

As with any creation, there have been many amazing people involved with this book behind the scenes. Without them I would not be here sharing this book with you now.

I could not have done this without the years of love and support from my wonderful husband, Henri – one of those enlightened men, determined to change the patriarchal world – and my amazing son, Alexander, just for being himself. I'd like to thank my parents, Ruth and David, for their love, for giving me all my educational opportunities, for always treating me and my brother as equals, never telling me I couldn't do something because I was a girl and always encouraging me to fulfil my highest potential. My gratitude also goes to the King's High School, Warwick, for encouraging me to study science and telling me to beat the men, and Jesus College Cambridge for the thirst for excellence and discovery I gained there.

There have been some very challenging times in my life and I probably wouldn't be here if it weren't for the love and friendship I've received. In particular, I want to thank my brother Steven, Manuella Jessop, Emma Anderson, Alpa Pabari, James Sargent, Gordon Banner, Verity Graydon and Mike Cherry for being the very best of friends.

I'm also grateful to the wonderful musicians Heather Wallace, Christine Edmundson and the members of Lyra Davidica, and Giles Turner and the members of the Kingfisher Chorale; I cannot imagine how my life would have been without the music. I am sure they don't realise just how much of a difference they made. I am also deeply grateful to the inspirational women Patricia Date, Philippa Merivale, Melissie Jolly, Moira Bush, Tamra Oviatt and Helen Lenygon.

A huge thank you to all my courageous clients and students over the last two decades, and the members of my Women's Empowerment Group, who weren't afraid to let me dig into their subconscious minds, to confront their beasts, to share their stories, to experience my radical healing techniques – often hot off the press – and in doing so helped me make the discoveries I'm able to share with you now.

ACKNOWLEDGEMENTS

I also want to thank Melanie Gow for helping me extract my true story and free myself from being labelled a bereaved mother; Rachel Elnaugh for writing the foreword; and Barbara Bogusz, Melissie Jolly, Dr Julia Goedecke, Moira Bush, Sophia Marsh-Ochsner, Marisa Murgatroyd and Korani Connolly for their valuable feedback and reviews. I'd also like to thank the team at Rethink Press, Lucy McCarraher, Kathleen Steeden and Abigail Willford; and Katy Wheatley for pushing me out onto social media.

I would like to thank each and every one of the people who helped to fund this book, and especially:

James Sargent, Prof David Whitehouse, Mrs Ruth Whitehouse, Steven Whitehouse, Mrs Christine Atkinson, Hema Patel, Sarah Morris, Anne-Marie Green, Michael Hillman, Pamela Strisofsky, Dr Henri Winand, Beau Bennett, Laura Steward, Lara Lallyette, Alpa Pabari, Magnus Almqvist, Anne Glover, Simmi Sethi, Victoria Luis, Penelope Nelson, Gisella McGuinness, Manuella Jessop, Sheena Thakrar, Katy Wheatley, Barbara Bogusz, Dr Julia Goedecke, Miss Deborah Brown, Dr Mary Ann Testarmata, Gill Rutter, Moira Andrews, Ann Goedecke and Helen Biswas.

I am enormously grateful for their faith in me, my work and my vision to transform the world for women.

Finally, I would like to thank you, my readers, for joining your energy with mine so we can shift the

227

group consciousness, deactivate the unconscious bias, heal Female History Syndrome, and create a world for our daughters where they are free to simply be themselves and be brilliant.

With love
Anne xx

An Interview With The Author

QUESTION: *If we were sitting here a year from now celebrating what a great year it's been for you, what would you have achieved?*

ANNE: I am on a mission to enable one million women worldwide to pull back their power and realise their full potential, so that they blossom in everyday life and achieve great things in their careers, without crippling stress, anxiety or lack of self-belief destroying their wellbeing. It's a mission to drive a new era of confident, amazing women who are truly free to shine powerfully.

Women don't currently have a level playing field, despite our official rights, and up until now the real underlying cause of this hasn't been identified. Without true understanding, there cannot be a solution. I believe I have found both the root of the problem and the solution. It is knowledge that can change the lives of many, many women.

This is the culmination of everything I've been working towards for more than two decades – to bring powerful insight, tools that work, and genuine freedom to the many women who are currently being held back from achieving everything of which they are capable.

I'm determined to communicate what I have discovered to the women who need to know. This knowledge, and these tools, can do far more than simply prevent other women going through what I did. They enable us to become more amazing than we ever imagined possible.

So, a year from now, we will be celebrating being well on the way to making that happen!

Q: You've said there was a critical turning point, a moment that defined everything which was to come. What was it?

A: It was back in my lecturer days, when my chronic fatigue was spiralling out of control and everything was falling apart. I remember lying on the sofa, with nothing but dismal daytime TV (back in the days before cable), literally too weak to move. I couldn't even move my arm and pick up a pen. My consultant had simply said he didn't know why I felt so ill, wished me luck and discharged me. I remember the despair, thinking that my life was essentially over, even though I was only thirty years old. That was the point in my life when The Beast had total control over me. If I had accepted what I'd been told, I would still be there.

However, in that moment something amazing happened. Deep in that pit of despair I made a conscious choice – like flipping a switch in my head. I chose to reject what I'd been told. I chose to believe that there was a solution which could help me get my life back again. I decided that I would make another reality for myself, even though I had no idea how to do it, or how long it would take. I chose to believe that all the official opinions were wrong, and that I could solve the problem for myself.

At the time, I knew nothing about the subconscious, our internal operating system, or what my mind had perceived in the world that had taken away my power and locked me into perpetual fight or flight. I simply chose to believe that a solution existed and that I was capable of finding it. I was right.

Although it was only a moment, I've thought about it many times since then. I know that by choosing to believe there was another option, I opened up the possibility for the knowledge, the opportunities and the path I needed, to come into my reality and manifest in my life.

Of course, the journey took many years, and a great deal of work, but that was the defining moment which enabled me to be here today. That was the fork in the road. That was the moment which brought me here with all this understanding, these tools, having transformed my own life and helped many women transform theirs.

Q: Who would you say has been the greatest influence on who you are? Who helped shape the values you have today?

A: Many people have inspired me over the years, but the person who without a doubt transformed me the most was my daughter Rebecca. In 2014, she passed away very suddenly in her sleep, at the age of seven.

Before she died, I had already found the true cause of my own burnout, the underlying subconscious Beast, and the understanding of Female History Syndrome, and I was beginning to develop the tools I needed to change it. I thought I'd been through my biggest trials. Little did I know!

When I found my little girl's body that terrible morning, my world shattered. It was a challenge simply to survive to the next moment.

I've lost count of the number of people who told me my life was ruined because my child had died. But I was only forty-five years old and wasn't prepared to accept that. For her, I couldn't let that be the end for me. I was determined that I would come through it and not only find joy again, but use the experience to create something phenomenal.

It was during this time that I realised I needed something beyond subconscious reprogramming techniques. I learnt first-hand that when you have lost your power foundation completely, are frozen in trauma and in zero power, changing your beliefs just isn't enough.

It was my desperation to come through the pain that drove me to think even further outside the box, and experiment in ways nobody had before. The breakthroughs in understanding, and developments in my techniques, that I made in the years after Rebecca's death were phenomenal. Not only that, but my original mission to empower women had transformed into a driving passion to free all women!

Out of the worst that life can bring, the hardest thing a woman can go through, came something so positive – and not just in her memory, not just for me but for women everywhere. Rebecca was a little spark of light. She was fearless, loving, totally empowered and so very different from me, with my stress and insecurities. Everyone who knew her commented on how much she lit up their lives. In many ways she was the epitome of feminine confidence. She knew she was enough and she shone effortlessly.

Losing her was the worst experience of my life, and yet, if I hadn't been through that, I wouldn't have the deep understanding of the human power matrix, or the techniques to influence it, that I'm bringing to you now.

Rebecca was all about freedom, femininity and expressing who she was. She would have found it delightful that her legacy, through me, is to help many other women to find that freedom.

Q: Other people are working to empower women and help them feel confident or were already doing this kind of work before you came along. What made you think there was something missing that you could do differently?

A: I didn't just think there was something missing, I knew there was!

Having practised all the standard techniques and trained in the most cutting-edge subconscious healing modalities I personally found that these things simply hadn't changed the way I felt, deep down, in stressful situations.

At the same time, year after year, despite being highly capable, women with the same patterns of burnout and low confidence came to me for help.

This is clearly a universal phenomenon which has not been addressed by the prevailing wisdom at all. Otherwise it would have been solved by now.

Here's the thing: if we don't understand exactly where we are and why, we simply cannot create an effective solution.

It's like wanting to get to London by train, and the world tells you that you need a ticket from a town a hundred miles away – here in the UK that could be Leicester, for example. You buy that ticket, but it doesn't actually work, so you buy another and try to get on the train again, and again it doesn't work – because it turns out you are actually in another city in another country, like Edinburgh in Scotland.

The problem is that you are much farther from your destination than the world realised.

Don't get me wrong, all the conventional empowerment work is of immense value and does produce results, up to a certain point. However, any woman who experiences these deep undermining patterns will only ever be plastering over the cracks with conventional techniques. It's the acknowledgement of where we really are, combined with the tools designed specifically for that starting point, which gets us to the destination we desire and deserve.

A ticket from Leicester to London will never get us from Edinburgh, Scotland, to London, England. It's as simple as that. I knew we were all missing something huge and I set out specifically to find it.

The proof of the pudding is in the eating! My theories are based on what I have identified in many people's minds over two decades; the conclusive evidence is that the same patterns come up again and again. The tools I have developed are focused on undoing this very specific disempowerment and creating a new foundation energy. I have experienced huge benefits myself, as have my clients. This is indeed new and different.

Q: Why does this matter to a woman in Topeka, in the state of Kansas in the United States, who wonders how this is relevant to her life?

A: It's relevant to all women. Female History Syndrome – the legacy of our historical disempowerment and the rapid opening up of opportunity – is felt by all women, wherever they are, whichever culture they find themselves in.

The extent to which it undermines us, and how we react, depends on our unique life experiences, our aspirations, our character and – most importantly – how much we are pulling away from the old patriarchal operating system. The limitations, energetic restrictions and blocks are there for us all.

No matter who you are, or where you're from, when you remove the subconscious straitjacket that all women are born into, your life will open up. You will experience less inner conflict, fewer blocks, greater wellbeing, less stress and more confidence. Everyone wants this, whether you're a full-time mother, a retail assistant, holding a role in the corporate world, an entrepreneur, or a professional like a lawyer or (like me) a scientist.

When women feel truly free to express their gifts and talents in the world, everyone benefits.

Q: What do you do when you are not building the power foundation with women everywhere, undoing 'generational conditioning' and snipping the threads of the 3D Spider's Web of Limitation?

A: My passion is singing, in particular, Renaissance music. On a Sunday evening you'll find me rehearsing with the wonderful Kingfisher Chorale, a chamber choir I've been a member of for nearly twenty years.

There's nothing better than bringing to life a stunning 500-year-old masterpiece of incredible beauty. I couldn't imagine my life without the music. My singing has been an enormous source of strength, inspiration and comfort to me, and kept me going through the most difficult times in my life.

Q: How did the 3D Spider's Web of Limitation first come to you?

A: It was actually back in 2012. I'd been struggling with my own hidden limits – I have them, just like any woman. At that point in my life, I was moving into group healing work, trying to be more visible and build my business, and this took me way out of my comfort zone. I'm naturally an introvert and don't feel a particular need to be in the limelight. I kept hitting block after block after block. Instead of giving up, or believing I was just not good enough, I did my usual thing, which is to dig and find the real cause of why this was happening.

I began to identify many subconscious limits around all areas of life, which my mind labelled as utterly forbidden for me to pass: limits relative to my husband, my family, my brother, my childhood, my ancestry, men in general, limits around money, success, freedom, social status, leadership. The list was endless, and all based on obsolete patriarchal and class beliefs, not on the opinions of the actual people in my life, or the way I had been brought up to think.

Prior to this, I had known about all the programmes and the old operating system but I hadn't realised that these create actual energetic blocks within us all.

It was these blocks that were stopping me moving forwards, as effectively as if I were in a straitjacket. Not only that, but each time I pushed one of these limits, it triggered huge anxiety, stress and health problems, and all my efforts ground to a halt.

Everyone has heard of the glass ceiling, but what I have identified is much greater than this. We are actually surrounded by an enormous number of limits in every imaginable direction. I saw that I was stuck in this huge invisible web. Every time I tried to move, I was pulled back to my original position.

The 3D Spider's Web could not be a more perfect analogy for what is actually happening to us under the surface.

Q: What three surprising things would someone who doesn't know you never guess about you?

A: That's easy! I'm an avid crocheter and my house is covered in crochet animals, so many in fact that you might think a toddler lived there. For me, though, it's a way of being deeply creative. It's both relaxing and satisfying. It's like a meditation for the hands, leaving the mind free to wander. In fact, it is while crocheting that I have made some of my biggest breakthroughs.

I'm also a huge fan of 1960s cult TV, especially *The Man from U.N.C.L.E.* 'Open Channel D!' This is a passion I discovered at the age of seven, and it's still with me decades later.

Six years ago, I decided to teach myself to play the lute. I often think I should have been born in sixteenth-century Venice, but then I remember the dying in childbirth, the plague and the total lack of women's rights, and I know I was born at exactly the time I was meant to be, to bring all this knowledge to today's women and free them from the legacy of the past.

Q: Is there a book, film, play or poem that has influenced your vision?

A: Believe it or not, I would say the film *The Matrix*. This came out right at the beginning of my journey when I was firmly rooted in the conventional world, before I had learnt any of my energy techniques or released any of my limiting beliefs.

The core concept – that we create our reality with our minds, and that logically, therefore, we can change the world when we expand our belief in what our minds can do – really inspired me. It was a very important seed that opened up many possibilities for me.

'There is no spoon!'

Q: If you had to narrow it down to one piece of advice for either a client or someone aspiring to 'be you' or to achieve what you have, what would that be?

A: Well, there have to be two pieces of advice. First, whatever has happened to you, instead of seeing yourself as a victim of life, turn it around. The biggest challenges give us a huge opportunity to learn, expand and grow. It is when we are pushed to the limit, that we find our true genius. So, make it your mission to find whatever that genius is for you, and it will help you come through your challenges, more amazing than you ever believed possible.

Second, never believe something is impossible, no matter how much the world around you says it is. While you believe it is impossible you will close down all possibility of creating it. Choose to believe that it is possible, and people simply haven't discovered the mechanism yet. Even better, tell yourself that *you* will be the one to discover how. Then do it!

Q: What's your next big move?

A: I've got several things planned. First, the expansion of my online empowerment membership, The Power Sanctuary, which I've designed to help women take the Six Keys I talk about in this book to a deeper level and receive more profound life shifts. Then I see myself running weekend events with hundreds of women, all ready to pull back their power, create their power foundation and activate their true brilliance.

Oh, and there's the next book, *Pull Back Your Money Power!*

Q: What would you like your readers to do now?

A: As a Life Alchemist, I help visionary women like you to reawaken your ancient intrinsic magic, to become the powerful Sorceress inside, and to create your own Energy Matrix Power Foundation that puts you on a truly level playing field, so you can embrace your fully faceted female power and effortlessly embody your highest vision for yourself.

I want this for you! The first step is to connect with me through my website at: www.feminineconfidence. com/pullbackyourpowerbonuses

There you'll find bonus audio meditations and clearings to help you with each of the Six Keys to Empowerment. This will help get you started on your journey straight away!

I also invite you to join my free Facebook community (you'll find the link on my website) where you can connect with other women on the same empowerment journey, and receive answers and support.

You will also be able to take things further with deep energy work, using my unique power healing techniques, if you feel this is right for you.

We are creating a new group consciousness where women are able to build the power foundation they have been missing for so long. The more of us come on board, the more established this new energy becomes, and the easier it is for us all to have and sustain it in our everyday lives. We are building a new world, and I'd love for you to be part of it.

You can find me online at:

⊕ www.feminineconfidence.com

🅵 www.facebook.com/annewhitehousephd